Praise for Su

ACCEPTANCE OF WHAT IS

I am writing this testimonial just as I finished reading your amazing book. It is now 3:01 a.m. I couldn't put it down. It was an amazing story of hope, faith and all things mommy hood. I really enjoyed your vulnerability and the way you took me with you in your journey. You have inspired me so much to never give up. Your book is going to help so many moms out there. Thank you for giving your son a voice and for never giving up.

—Angie Robinson

Unashamed of bearing the rawness of her soul and spirit, Nicola Irvine takes us (her dear readers) on the decades long journey of being a special needs mum to her precious son, Thomas. From the knee-jerk reaction to wanting to "fix" him to ultimately acknowledging him as perfect, whole and complete is a powerful journey that reminds us to lean into the silent moments, honor what IS and stay present to the never-ending messages of the limitless possibilities of the universe. *Surrender* is a must read for anyone seeking spiritual reminders that EVERYTHING is FOR us. The good, the bad, the ugly and the uncomfortable – every situation is an opportunity for our own awakening. May we all lean into the deeper spiritual messages for each of us!

—Susanna Peace Lovell,
Life Coach & Disability Rights Activist

I couldn't wait to pick up *Surrender* each day. It gives me hope that nothing in this journey is permanent. My daughter and I are continuing to evolve and grow. This journey gets better as we learn and become more in touch with ourselves and our Higher Power.

—Carrie Hunsucker, Our Exceptional Tribe

As a professional I strongly urge other professionals to read this book and to open to possibilities that might not have been in our evidence based teachings and clinical best practices. As a speech therapist I feel our fundamental role is to support communication, and yet at its core what this generates is simply connection. Thomas forced many of us to explore unique ways of finding this, and Nicola has modelled the immense courage it takes to be in true surrender, compassion and advocacy of a soul that came into her guardianship for a speck of time on this universe.

—Tracy-Kim Gilchrist,
B. Speech Pathology and Audiology,
M. Alternative and Augmentative Communication

This powerful story shows us all how to create inspiring possibilities and find loving acceptance no matter what challenge is thrown at us. Nicola and her son Thomas are shining lights for this world.

—Rachael Jayne Groover,
author of Powerful and Feminine.

SURRENDER

A mother's acceptance of what is

NICOLA IRVINE

ISBNs
Paperback: 978-1-64184-787-2
Ebook: 978-1-64184-788-9

Book Design: JETLAUNCH
Cover Design: Bronya Rhind-Eglese

TABLE OF CONTENTS

PART TWO: GIFTS WITHIN MY JOURNEY AND HOW TO

PART THREE: CONVERSATIONS WITH THOMAS

PREFACE

I am a New Zealander who has lived on four continents. I have made a conscious choice to write in New Zealand English. I hope my American readers and friends will see beyond the additional u's, the s's instead of z's and other spelling differences to obtain their insights from within Thomas's and my journey.

INTRODUCTION

Welcome, dear reader

The reason you have this book in your hand is you know it is time to make a change in your life so that you can live your purpose, enjoy the juice in life, and learn to live again. It is your soul that has drawn you to this book. Your soul is wanting you to lighten your load, take out the bricks in your backpack, and allow your joy to flow. It is time to find your heart again and be connected to your soul.

Maybe you have had a crisis in your life, hit a brick wall, had some kind of spiritual wake-up call, or perhaps you are like me: you have climbed the wrong mountain, collected emotional baggage in your backpack along the way, and then when the mountain started to crumble, you realised you really wanted to be on the mountain over in the distance. And it has taken me a few wake-up calls and decades to know this.

My desire is to assist you, the dear reader, to fast-track back to your heart, your purpose, and your soul. This is why I decided to write this book with huge encouragement from my son, Thomas. Know that I do not regret my past experiences, as I know I wouldn't be the person I am today had all of those experiences not occurred. Yes, I embrace the good, the bad, and the ugly or as I recently heard, "the good, the bad, and the godly." I love the person I am today. It hasn't been easy and indeed I have struggled with surrendering and accepting what has happened to me. I had suppressed my emotions. I had lived by my human ego, only to find there is an easier way to do life. It is to be. To be me. The "me" right in the core of my being.

Over these few decades, I have tried, tested and learned numerous techniques, teachings, and therapies. Some are more beneficial than others and some still remain as part of my daily practices for my health and well-being today. One of my key techniques has been to go through what I call "the valley of emotions." The first mountain I climbed in my life was a mountain of striving, lots of pushing and accumulating material things. I eventually realised, it was not the mountain I wanted to be on. I wanted to be on the mountain in the distance, the mountain where my heart was open, my soul was singing, and I was living my purpose. What I needed to do was to be aware of my emotions, allow my emotions and feel my emotions in their rawest of states, and not attach a story to my emotions. As a young woman, I did not really feel my emotions, so there has been much for me to let go and remember. I needed to remember that emotions are just the pure energy, energy in motion. When you allow your emotions without attaching a story, they pass very quickly.

In the past, I was determined, single-minded and a striver. I would say I lived purely in my ego. That's why I believe I have had numerous spiritual wake-up calls to awaken me to my true purpose, passion, and my soul.

As you read about my spiritual wake-up calls, you will read about how I discovered that in feeling my emotions, defeating my fears, I am now able to live my purpose. I now want to inspire you to do the same.

As I connected more with being, I was able to connect more directly with Thomas. I realised that within Thomas's challenges, there was a gift. I also recognised that others like Thomas need an advocate, a parent or caregiver, who is listening, present, and connected to their heart to assist and bring their gift to the surface.

This book is to assist you to do this. To assist you to open your heart so you can listen, and have what I have with my son, Thomas. Thomas makes it clear this book is to ultimately assist others like him. The way to do this is help their parents and caregivers gain the peace, the calm and purpose they crave so they can learn to live again.

Thomas is perfect just the way he is. He is 23-years-old, soon to be living in his own home, an internet business owner, a social being who happens to be bilaterally profoundly deaf, he has epilepsy, is left side hemiplegia, developmentally delayed, and non-verbal. He, along with Alicia, Siân, and Greg, have taught me to be the best person I can be.

Your Thomas is offering you this same opportunity. All you need to do is STOP. Listen to what your soul is wanting for you.

DEDICATION

To my children

Thomas … you are my teacher who guides and reminds me who I am and what I am born to be … me.

Alicia, Siân, and Greg … In the past eight years, you have assisted me to truly understand unconditional love beyond the bounds of blood.

I love you.

Thank you. Thank you. Thank you.

PART ONE

My Journey

AM I GOING CRAZY?

Am I going crazy? I think.

"Is that you, Thomas?" I ask.

"*Yes, Mummy. It's me,* Thomas replies.

My mind is trying to work this out. In the past, I had spoken to Thomas telepathically but the clarity at which he is coming through this time shocks me.

I just wasn't expecting this.

"So lovely to connect with you, my dear," I say to Thomas.

It's like I have a totally clear line. There is no interference, it's not muffled. There is a clear and direct channel to my son.

"I know. I feel so relieved I can reach you this way. I have been waiting for such a long time for you to allow the disturbances, the patterns, the conditioning of life to fall away so we could have clear communication between us," Thomas explains.

As I hear this from Thomas, my previous thoughts, of you going crazy, Nicky, and no one will believe you, seem to fade away into the distance.

I can finally hear him clearly.

"I can hear you loud and clear, my darling boy."

The truth is part of me feels crazy. Yet I know it is clear direct communication from Thomas.

We have tried so many different ways to communicate that have led to exhaustion, sheer frustration, and outright disappointment. So much hard work. So much energy ...

So much effort ... So much money ... Blood, sweat, as well as tears.

All I really needed to do was clear out all of my patterns, struggles, beliefs, and conditioning to allow clear communication with my son, who is unable to speak. In saying this, I need to be aware of all my patterns, struggles, beliefs, and conditioning so in any moment I know I have a choice of how to react or not, as the case maybe. Later in this book, I share about my daily practices which assist me to live more in this way. It sounds so easy: just clear out all my patterns, struggles, beliefs, and conditioning. For some people it may be easy, but the clearing process work has taken me on quite an adventure.

At this time, Thomas can say a few words. He can ask you to "look, come, drink, or eat" and he can most definitely ask you for his favourite band, *"The Wiggles"* an Aussie children's band to be played on his iPad or nearest television. *"The Wiggles"* have soothed Thomas and me in many very stressful moments over the past two decades. Thomas's words also include "yummy," which means food; or there's McDonald's nearby and Thomas just wants to let you know he realises that; "car" which means, "Let's get out of here" (generally when he is at his home) and go for a ride in my car or yours if that is what he wants. Thomas points, he grabs your hand or arm or even guides your head to get you to focus on what he wants you to focus on. Less favourably, he will behave in a way that demands your attention right there and then. He has definitely tried to teach me it is best to listen to him the first time. Waiting or patience is not one of his strong points. And I need to say, not mine, either.

WHO ARE YOU TO SHARE HIS STORY?

Many years ago, I took Thomas to an osteopath's treatment. This osteopath had been treating Thomas since he was 18 months-old. I shared with him that I would like to share Thomas's story. He looked at me as if to say, "Who are you to share his story?" At that time and place, he was delivering a message from God. It was true. I wasn't in a space to be able to understand, accept, and have compassion for any of what Thomas's journey was about. That said, I was so affronted by his comment at the time, but I knew he spoke the truth. There has been so much learning since that day in his treatment room; I am able to understand and communicate with Thomas at a deeper level. A place where words are not required. I don't always like what I hear. I sometimes feel upset, and sad for the things done or said to him in the past. At least now I know and have the ability to forgive and have compassion for myself. I just was doing the best I could with the tools I had at the time. It was how it was going to be at that time. Acceptance of what it was and indeed what it is, was one of the key elements for me.

"So, Thomas, here I am. In service of you and in service of your readers. What is it you would like to share? What is it you would like me to share about the journey, your journey?"

YOU CAN

"You know you can, Mummy. It is all within you. This book has been written already. It just needs to be typed and shared in whichever way possible. You have to be my channel for this. The timing is divine. It is the best possible time for this book to be birthed. I trust that you will be able to deliver the message of love, of unconditional love, and the search for the meaning of your life. You have to remember who you are and why you are here. You have messages of my soul. Your ego/personality/humanness has been worked on and now there is awareness of these different aspects of yourself. It's not that your ego/personality/humanness will not venture out again. Indeed, there will be times when you will require it and it will be totally appropriate at that particular moment.

The universe needs my messages ... messages of trust ... trust in self ... the inner knowingness.

Everyone needs to STOP, be still and open their heart to the possibilities. This is not possibilities of the mind but possibilities of the universe. There are an infinite number of possibilities and potential. You are going to be the deliverer of this message to your readers. The readers may in turn choose to share their message as well.

The message is a message of faith in self, in the wisdom of God/the universe/the divine presence that embraces you and leads you to divine possibilities. We all have this potential even those of us who have chosen to do things differently or have more challenge in this life. This is our choice. It is my choice.

Now you accept this. Now you know this to be true, you can be a perfect messenger for me. You can do this, Mummy. This is your purpose. I know you know this.

You can do it."

THE NIGHT BEFORE

The night before my writers' retreat, I can hear Thomas so clearly, as if he were talking to me in person, in the same room.

"You can do it, Mum.

It is your time, Mum.

This is divine timing, Mum.

It is time for you to tell my story from the beginning. You have worked so tirelessly allowing you and me to arrive at this particular point in time."

I have tears running down my face. I notice Thomas is now calling me Mum, not Mummy … I wonder why for a moment and then it passes.

I think, how can I do this? How will I know what Thomas wants me to write?

Just as I think this, Thomas replies, *"Mum, you know what you think and feel. You also know how I think and feel. You are so connected to me. I want you to write this book for me and for all the others who don't have the words, the voice or the ability to write or type. This is your purpose."*

My tears had stopped only to start again. The tears gather at the tip of my nose until there are enough there to allow them to fall. A constant stream of tears. I can't believe there are so many of them. Where are they coming from? I question myself. Answer: from a the deepest well of sadness, grief, joy, and love.

Then as I became aware of the fact I had been crying for some time, I am overwhelmed by light. Such a feeling of peace floods my being. I am in awe of the stillness it brings to me.

"Okay, Thomas. You have me. I will. I can write what you would like me to write for you." I spoke so softly and tenderly as I am still in awe of what had just transpired.

"But can I sleep now so I am ready for my writers' retreat tomorrow?"

I could feel Thomas nod his head.

"Thank you."

I take a deep breath in and ask my Divine Author Within the time and space to allow me to rest and sleep well overnight. Just before I go to sleep, I am taken by a visualisation of a Skype call with Thomas and his two support workers. He is in the happiest of spaces. I can feel his joy, his contentment of what just happened. My heart opens wider falling into a peaceful, calm night of bliss.

I woke feeling so refreshed, having a proverbial spring in my step. It was as if a fresh start was here. The night before, I had written a contract with myself about my intentions for fulfilling my soul's purpose. My whole being was in resonance with my contract ... the possibilities, the path that was appearing. The contract included a simple yet nurturing morning routine to nurture my whole being ... mind, body, and soul. I was in the best possible place, physically, mentally, emotionally, socially, and spiritually to commence my new project, my first book via the Tom Bird Method ... my third actual book.

Just before I sprang out of bed, I felt drawn to my iPhone. I had been making it a practice not to check my iPhone until I had completed my morning routine, but I couldn't stop myself. I just had to look at it.

I skimmed my emails. I could see there was an email from Thomas's email account. Thomas is not able to use a computer or send emails, but his support workers can.

The email included a card reading. A card reading is when Thomas connects with the energy of friends and family via their photos. He connects directly with their heart and selects a card from the decks he uses and what we have found is, the reading resonates directly to what is happening in their life, in their heart. This is his gift. I have shared about his gift in my second book *Communication His Way*.

So, this very morning Thomas had completed a spontaneous card reading for me overnight. I was so keen to read it, as his readings were always so insightful – verging on spooky because it was as if he were in my head and heart. So, this morning's reading was a card from the animal pack created by Steven Farmer. Normally, a reading would include a photo of the person (in this case me) having the reading plus the card/s chosen by Thomas. In this particular situation, Thomas's support worker had taken a photo of all the readings together and a photo of each individual card not a photo of me and the card/s selected by Thomas.

Have a look at the card above. My interpretation of the above card was that Thomas knew I have everything I need in order to move forward with my purpose, my life purpose. I felt he was reassuring me. It was time to go forth and share his story, his words and wisdom, with the world. Ready or not, world, it is time.

I had to trust I had the skills to keep my personality, my ego totally out of it so I could share his words in the purest form aligned with his intentions.

WOW. What an honour! Thomas was trusting me to share his words.

LEARNING TO LISTEN

Little did I know, all the self-development, self-inquiry work I had done was preparing me to be able to listen more clearly ... to the words of wisdom from within me and beyond and to the words from others, especially my son, Thomas. There were times in the past that I could have sworn I heard him speak to me, but I wasn't sure. I was full of doubt, always wanting to get validation from some other source. I was not trusting myself as often as my soul desired me to.

I had always thought I was a visual learner. I could only retain things when I wrote them down from a book or the teacher's blackboard ... not sure if many of the younger generation would know what a blackboard was. Anyway, I also understood information when there was a flow chart or bullet points.

I still need to say any information, whether numbers, names, or texts numerous times, before I can retain the information. It's just the way I am.

With all the transformational tools, therapies, and healings, and maybe just being older, wiser, an auditory pathway to a divine intelligence or wisdom appeared to have cleared and is opened to receive more than ever before. I realise this will be a continual process for the rest of my days. I don't type this in heaviness or as a burden, it is a way I am being in service of my gifts.

In the past, I have had messages from the other side. What I mean from the other side is messages from people who had passed away. There have been many messages, but I will share two of them with you. They had a significant impact on me, and perhaps the people I had to deliver the messages to. Perhaps, it was also the fact the messages could be validated, and they were delivered and received with the intention of being in service and with love.

In one of these two incidents, my brother-in-law contacted me to pass on a message to his brother, Thomas's dad, Bill. I believe the message gave a level of peace to Bill. I know there was scepticism there just as I know there is a sceptic in me, too.

In the other incident, a friend of Bill's, Thomas' dad had passed away a year prior before. His spirit contacted me sharing his concern for the partner he left behind. He asked that I contact Bill, asking him to check how his partner was, as she was in a relationship that wasn't good for her. Bill did as I asked and sure enough, she was in a relationship that wasn't good for her and thankfully the relationship had ended. His partner was shocked by his message. We met and discussed my encounter with him. She wanted so much more from him and me but nothing else was offered from him. I know it was frustrating for her and me. We needed to accept that it was complete. It was just a gentle hello from his spirit letting his partner know she was being looked after.

I am grateful Bill's deceased friend contacted me so we could ensure his partner was safe and well. Knowing she was being cared for from the other side gave her a lot of peace.

I am learning to listen, listen in a different way. It wasn't this way back in the day.

BACK IN THE DAY

When I was a young girl, our family lived on a small farm at Kaka Point, a small town south of Balclutha in South Otago, New Zealand. The farm was right opposite the South Pacific Ocean. I could walk out the front gate over the main road to the beach. When I say main road, the road only serves about 100 permanent residents and holiday makers who come to visit the area, as there is quite beautiful scenery. It was a very small sleepy town those five decades ago.

I have a lot of wonderful memories on the beach, doing as children do, building sandcastles, hunting for crabs under rocks, looking for fish in the rock pools, generally being inquisitive about everything, even the seaweed and the larger pieces of kelp. My grandad would cut out shoes from the kelp. Fun times, but I didn't care for the feel of the kelp beneath my feet. The ocean offered so many possibilities of exploring and creativity.

I don't remember swimming in that particular ocean which seems crazy, as now when the conditions are right, I love swimming in the ocean. Or maybe I did swim as I didn't feel the cold water like I do now. Having lived in Asia for 24 years, I have become accustomed to the more temperate waters Asia has to offer.

As a child I do remember swimming in the local rivers and lakes, but not the ocean. I just got in and tried it. Over the years, I became more cautious in terms of swimming. My time in Asia probably spoiled me. Thomas is totally like me, preferring the more temperate ocean in Asia.

My Mum and Dad wanted to offer my sisters and I the best possible education they could afford. I know they did without so we could have the opportunity to attend a boarding school only one hour away. Four decades ago, one hour by car seemed a huge distance. It wasn't thought possible to drive it daily yet in today's world, it would happen frequently, if not daily. So, it was decided, that being the eldest, I would be the first to attend at the tender age of 11.

Columba College provided much for me. An opportunity to bloom in a safe and secure environment. I found the environment great, especially in the first few years. I was really fortunate to have a teacher in my first two years of boarding school, who showed belief in me. In New Zealand, the years I talk about were called Form 1 and Form 2 … I was aged 11 and 12. I thrived under her guidance and teaching methods. I loved creative writing, remembering that I scored well in the assignments, which only inspired me to work harder and achieve more. I ended up having a very successful first two years at Columba, academically, in sports, and caring for others in community. I had so much self-belief and self-esteem. Everything and anything felt possible.

Unfortunately, it was in the next two years her belief in me was contradicted by my English teacher telling me I wasn't "good" at English. I took her perception to heart, creating a very strong belief that I wasn't good at this subject, so I turned my focus to other subjects. I also translated this belief into meaning that I wasn't good at writing or speaking in public. On one hand it was so sad, as it has taken me several decades to face the fear of not being good enough to write a book and craft a speech and deliver it on stage. As I write this, I know on the other hand that this very strong belief served me to be great with numbers and I now have the passion to deliver compelling stories through my books or motivational speeches on stage.

My years at Columba were a time of extreme challenge too … feeling abandoned and not knowing how to truly express it, feel it and let it go. I didn't share with anyone how I felt really about being at Columba although Mum and Dad must have known, with the way I addressed the envelopes of my weekly letters. From: Nicola Clark, Columba Colditz, Highgate, Dunedin. Colditz is a town in East Germany where during the World War II allied prisoners of war were held.

It was how I felt. I am sure it must have been upsetting for my parents. It wasn't spoken about. Deep within my being, I knew it was the right place for me, but that didn't make it an easy ride at times.

When I mention the word boarding school, I have a sense of not belonging. I was told I was too good. I wasn't going to fit in appropriately. It seems that the school had a policy of sending students away who they deemed wouldn't fit in. It was easier to suggest this cause of action to parents than rather assist a student to adapt….

I remember Mum and Dad having an appointment with my principal, although I don't remember if I was in the room or not, or what was discussed. I do remember getting the grit between my teeth and wanting to prove my principal and my school wrong, so I became resourceful as to how I was going to cope. Not that this was a conscious thought process but in a subconscious way, I started to build strategies to cope with being different, being too good for this particular boarding-school environment.

I just worked harder, faster, better. I didn't feel what I was feeling. I just got on by doing and achieving. When I felt a bit low, a bit down, I just picked myself up and got on with it. I would go, grab my tennis racket and hit a tennis ball against one of the brick walls around the school or grab a netball (netball is a ball sport played by two teams of seven players. Games are played on a rectangular court with raised goal rings at each end) and shoot goals or hide in an office where I could study without being disturbed. This was my coping strategy at school. Little did I know, it would catch up with me.

Later in my teenage years while still at Columba, I was like any other teenager, I wanted to buck the system. Not in the way most of the girls wanted to. They would leave the school premises without permission to go shopping or meet boys from the local schools. The way I wanted to buck the system was I wanted to challenge the rules, the principles that I thought were outdated or just outright stupid from my teenage perspective.

I do remember one particular rule: girls must wear skirts to dinner on a Saturday night. I thought this rule sucked, given fashion and times had moved on ... We were living in the 1980's. Gauchos pants are a fashionable ladies clothing item. At the time my mum had a retail-fashion shop, so I knew. Anyway, I decided to make my point by taking my turn to stand by the dining-room doors holding the doors open to enable everyone, including the house matrons and leaders, into the dining room for dinner. Of course, I was seen. Of course, I was told off by the head of house how inappropriate it was to wear gauchos. It was not acceptable not to follow the rules. In the moment, I believe I offered my perspective and asked if we could agree to disagree. I don't remember if I pushed this rule again or not, but this experience is ingrained in my psyche.

I loved that when I was pushed, I felt I needed to push back. It was important to me. I knew I had the push if I needed to push. I just didn't know at the time how much I would need "the push" when it came to advocate for Thomas and all he required in life.

In the last year of my school education, prior to attending University to study for a bachelor's degree, I was one of the girls who drank alcohol on the school premises before attending our 6th and 7th form formal dance. I can't remember how we got the alcohol into our dormitories, but we did. It was something I tried and tasted but wouldn't have had more than a half glass if indeed my consumption was more than a couple of mouthfuls. Whatever the amount I had, I had consumed alcohol. Telling the truth about this event and my involvement got me suspended from school for a week.

If truth be known, although embarrassed about getting into trouble (my sisters were secretly so happy as they now had some flexibility with what Mum and Dad would accept from them. Being the eldest, I had broken-in my parents to some teenage behaviour), my suspension meant a week at home with my family, assisting Mum in her shop. I actually enjoyed this time away from school hanging out with Mum….

It didn't take long for everyone to know what had happened. It felt like it was my whole world. Even my aunt and uncle, who lived a five-hour drive away, found out, prior to my parents or me being able to tell them. Bush telegraph worked well in the South Island of New Zealand. Partly embarrassed, partly a badge of honour that I too could push different boundaries.

I remember all the senior-year students were being interviewed individually by the principal. Fortunately, before I had my interview, I had time to telephone my mum to ask for some advice. It was the most important advice. "Tell the truth, Nicky. Otherwise, the lie will be with you for the rest of your life." Thank you, Mum. To this day, honesty and integrity remain two of my top values. So, I prepared myself and told the truth. And was suspended for drinking in the dorms prior to our formal dance.

A week with my family, assisting my mum in her clothing shop. What a punishment. I secretly enjoyed the time away from school. I really didn't want to be at school anymore. I felt I was ready to get on with the next step ... not sure I really knew what the next step should be but off to university it was, along with my other school friends. That young teenager with strong views on rules is still a part of me today.

Interestingly enough, my school made a huge effort to get us all back early as we were to participate in a sports tournament in Christchurch ... about a five-hour bus ride away. You see, all of us who were suspended were in the top sports teams. The school didn't want to go without us as my school would certainly have lost the tournament. I don't remember the result of the tournament, I just remember the process of getting there.

From my perspective, it was a lesson to me about how two-faced a school could be and indeed, life could be. In order to keep up appearances they needed us to play in the sports tournament. Was it about saving face? Saving reputation? I am not sure. I do remember two other girls not getting suspended like the rest of us. What I remember was, it was because of their parents' influence. I found that fascinating, how there were different rules for different people. An insight into the injustice of the world. Sometimes life just isn't fair.

I held onto this for years. The injustice. I held a lot of resentment toward my principal and my school board, and the way they dealt with the whole suspension situation. I was incensed by the injustice.

Maybe that is why I ended up serving on a school board as a community representative. Although I don't think that as board members, we were involved so heavily in matters like this.

My resentment kept building as years passed. I didn't understand it at the time. It became so strong that I ended up approaching the principal on a school visit a decade later, telling her how I didn't feel she treated me appropriately. I didn't give her the opportunity to respond. I just said what I needed to say, turned, and left. I felt free of that resentment. I was able to let it go, forgive her from a place deep within me and move forward. It was incredible.

Nowadays, I don't wait decades to feel the feelings that have been triggered. I am able to let the emotion pass (most of the time). I don't hold onto resentment. I don't allow the resentment to fester. I use a technique called a campfire process. More about that in a later chapter. It was a tool I was going to use extensively in my life, especially when it came to my spiritual wake-up calls.

SPIRITUAL WAKE-UP ONE: UNKNOWN WORLD OF PARENTHOOD

Although there are books out there, and information on the internet, no one can really prepare you for parenthood. I really didn't know how I would react to motherhood. Several months into it, it seemed that I was settling into motherhood well, until one day out of the blue, when my world got thrown upside down. My family was thrown into a cocktail mixer, not stirred but shaken viciously and poured out, to live a different way of life, totally foreign to the life I had known. The skills I had gained from the nine-and-a-half months preceding needed to be thrown out. I was in a new paradigm. It felt like it was time to start from scratch, a new beginning.

What I am writing about is when Thomas contracted pneumococcal meningitis in 1998 at the tender age of nine-and-a-half months and nearly died. Life as I knew it was over although this wasn't an instant knowing. It became a learned knowing that took years to grasp.

What has become obvious is there are different ways to deal with grief. The situation I found myself in was so foreign to me. It was like everyone was speaking in a totally different language. I didn't have a guide or phrase book. I coped with the fear, the stress, and grief by becoming the crusader, the fixer, with a desire to search out whatever therapy, book, expert to make Thomas better. Return Thomas back to the way he was.

This crusade, this wanting to fix, the desire to make him the way Thomas was before, took Thomas and I to many places over the world.

One of the most amazing experiences was spending three weeks in Abadiania, Brazil, visiting John of God. This took a lot of organising. Thankfully we had a New Zealand guide who knew the ropes and the trip happened without much drama. Thomas, me, and Thomas's two caregivers flew from Hong Kong to join a group in Auckland to fly to Rio de Janeiro and then on to Brasilia, where we bused to Abadiania. Thankfully, this wasn't a continuous journey. We did rest a few nights in Rio de Janeiro to enjoy the sights there before arriving at our pousada (a family-run guest house, like a bed and breakfast but all meals were provided) in Abadiania, Brazil, where it would be our home for the next three weeks. We easily fell into our simple, daily routine, which incorporated visits to the healing centre, known as the Casa, on the days it was opened. It was open three days a week. Dressed in white, we would walk to the Casa to receive guidance and follow it. The guidance was to either join the meditation rooms, have a crystal bed, or be in the operation room for spiritual surgery.

Both Thomas and I received much healing as I am sure Thomas's two caregivers did.

Prior to visiting John of God, Thomas was having about 100 seizures per day. During the three weeks, Thomas's seizures dropped significantly. This was a success for me. Because of the reduced seizures, Thomas became more engaged in the world in his environment in a way that was so wonderful to see. Also, he experienced being in the meditation rooms. They called them the "current" rooms. Thomas actually sat in one of these rooms for more than an hour. This was like a mini-miracle in itself as it was totally unheard of for Thomas to be so still. He was always a boy on the move. The sense was that he wanted to explore as much as he could. So, for him to experience this stillness was important for him.

As I mentioned, I believe I received healing as well. I spent time in the meditation rooms and also numerous crystal beds. Crystal beds are normal beds. There is a tripod that has seven arms with crystals at the end of each arm. The crystal bed operator will place the seven arms over each of your seven chakras: your crown, your third eye, your throat, your heart, your solar plexus, your sacral and your base. I was recommended to have a crystal bed several times while we were in Abadiania, as was Thomas. Thomas and I enjoyed our time in the crystal bed so much that we decided to buy one and bring it home with us. We still have it to this day.

My healing came in the form of realising the need to slow down my pace in life. This was indeed the first time I felt stillness. This was quite a realisation for me. I felt the pure joy of lying in a hammock for an hour. I had never been so still. Also, my healing was by way of "spiritual surgery," where it felt like someone was working with my reproductive system. I was sitting in a meditation room, the others in the room were sitting there too, no one was physically touching me, yet I could feel pushing and pulling in the lower part of my torso. After this healing I had to rest for over twenty-four hours. I was totally washed out. My legs could not carry me anywhere. Fortunately, our guide brought me soup and water to sustain me until I was able to get around and move the following day. Even Thomas knew to give me time to rest.

Thomas and I left Abadiania with fewer seizures, less emotional baggage and less expectations. We had developed an understanding and actual experience of stillness and how we yearned for more stillness in our lives.

Another overseas adventure took Thomas, my dad, Thomas's caregiver, and me to Los Angeles, USA. This was when Thomas was around three years old. We spent three weeks at the John Tracy Clinic there. At the time, the John Tracy Clinic offered a summer programme for out-of-state and overseas young children who had a hearing loss.

This was during the time I was really trying to fix Thomas. From my perspective, he was going to learn to speak just like his hearing peers. The meningitis had left Thomas with bilaterally profound deafness. He was given a cochlear implant when he was 14 months old. This was something Thomas's dad, Bill and I had to fight for, as many on the cochlear-implant funding committee didn't believe he should receive one. I believe their reasons were based on Thomas's poor MRI scans and what they deemed his potential to be. Fortunately, Thomas's paediatrician advocated strongly for him ... His message to them was "If anyone can, Thomas Pearson can," as he had been amazed by Thomas's development since his first examination of him. I am truly so thankful for his advocacy. The cochlear implant certainly gave Thomas the tool to learn language. He has some spoken words ... thanks to the cochlear implant. But for whatever reason, now at 23 years old, Thomas chooses not to wear the cochlear implant at all. Being an adult, this is his choice. Truthfully, I still wish he would choose to wear it, as I feel he would pick up more language, but I respect his decision and know he will not do anything he does not want to do.

Our time at the John Tracy Clinic was a time for Thomas to attend classes and therapy in normal preschool hours, for all of us to bond with other families who had children with hearing impairment, talk to experts at the clinic and to enjoy the sights, sounds, and scenes around Los Angeles. It included the usual things like Disneyland, shopping, and beaches.

It was wonderful to share this experience with my dad. He participated in discussions. He shared his story and vulnerability; as a result, many others benefited. It was an emotionally healing time for all of us. Thank you, Dad.

To top the adventure off with a bit of drama, unbeknown to us, Thomas had helped my dad pack his bag by putting a fresh orange into his checked-in bag. It was found by the New Zealand Ministry of Agriculture when he arrived home at New Zealand. I can imagine my dad's surprise to see the orange there, knowing he hadn't packed it. Fortunately, they believed his story that his grandson had packed it, not him, and he didn't have to pay a fine.

Thomas was keeping us on our toes!!

This unknown world was full of adventure. I was driven to fix Thomas, perhaps even create a new, better version and determined not to leave any stone unturned.

NO STONE UNTURNED ... TRYING EVERYTHING

Feeling let down by the medical profession, I sought answers in different places. Some less traditional, more contemporary therapies were explored. This was a world that was totally unknown to me at that time. Yet I was drawn to search for answers in any direction. I searched for the why. Why had this tragedy, this trauma (as this is how I saw it at that time) had happened to Thomas? Or maybe it was the search for relief from the fear, grief, and pain I was trying to cover up by being in control, wearing a mask, and being a super mum. I don't know really. I was searching and seeking for relief and answers that made sense to my mind.

I had known about chiropractors since I was at boarding school, as a friend's mum had discussed going to one for her sore back. At that time, I had never needed one, so I didn't have any direct experience with a chiropractor.

Thomas and I explored so many different therapies. Initially, my ultimate aim was to get my young boy back, the young boy I thought he would have been. How on earth did I think I knew how he would be? At that time, I believed I knew and that was the motivating force that got me out of bed. To fix, remake, rebuild my young boy, Thomas.

If anyone mentioned a therapy or a practitioner to me, I would research them, look at testimonials, gain understanding of what it was and what made it different from everything else I had experienced. I nominated myself to be the guinea pig for Thomas. I wanted to know what each therapy did and felt like, so I could anticipate what might the impact on Thomas might be. So, I could plan and control what Thomas was going through. Yes, the control freak was in full action.

In my first book, *Trust Life's Journey* I listed all the different therapies we explored.

Since publishing that book, we have explored more therapies, techniques, and anything that resonates deeply with me or that Thomas directs me to. Fortunately, the pace has relaxed. The seeking and searching have relaxed. I can see the synchronicity as it unfolds. Most of the time, Thomas and I are both able to breathe in and breathe out and live in the moment.

I know that each and every therapy and technique has had a purpose in Thomas's and my journey to get us where we are today. I want to acknowledge our practitioners for the part they played in Thomas's and my stories.

During July and August, 1998, Thomas was in two Hong Kong hospitals for about six weeks. Thomas's dad and I knew that once he was out of hospital and well enough to fly, we wanted to get him to New Zealand for a second opinion on his diagnosis, prognosis and for therapy. Thomas's diagnoses were bilaterally profound deafness, global developmental delay, epilepsy, and hemiplegia with uncertain outcome. Because Thomas had hydrocephalus immediately after meningitis, a VP shunt is inserted in his brain to drain extra cerebrospinal fluid, so when Thomas was given the "all clear" from the doctor to fly from Hong Kong to New Zealand, Thomas, his dad, Bill and me were on that plane.

My aunt was one of the first people to see Thomas once we arrived in Auckland, New Zealand. At the time, she was working in a chiropractic clinic about two-and-a-half hour's drive from Auckland, in Tauranga. She totally believed in the healing powers of the body and that the potential and possibilities were within the body, given what she had witnessed at the clinic where she worked. Also, she trusted her own intuition and knowing. This self-trust and inner wisdom planted a seed for me, guiding me down the path of self-trust and using my own intuition.

This encounter started our journey into the complementary, alternative, or anything other than traditional medicine. I will note here I believe there is a time and place for traditional medicine. Thomas is still on anti-epileptic medication and visits hospitals when there is an acute medical issue. I also believe in well-being, good nutrition, and listening to your body.

The journey taken by Thomas and me to chiropractors started initially in Tauranga. It was a great time to spend time with family there, as well as visit the clinic where my aunt worked. As I could feel the trust building within me, trust that what they did was somehow working for Thomas and me, I was able to accept a referral to a chiropractor in Auckland. This meant less travel which was good in one sense, but it meant we saw less of our family in Tauranga.

The Auckland chiropractor was only minutes away from our Auckland home, which saved Thomas and me travel time and it meant we could fit the chiropractic visit in as often as needed. It was through this chiropractor that I was introduced to his wife, who practised Reiki, energy-healing work. Reiki supported Thomas and me immensely. So much so, that I learned Reiki level 1 and 2 a few years later. The healing benefits from Reiki were incredible. Some of the benefits were very visible to the eye, but other benefits were not. I remember one particular time while visiting Thomas's paternal grandparents, Thomas fell out of his high-chair, hitting his head on the tile flooring. Yes … ouch.… Even though the incident was well over 18 years ago, just typing that still makes me cringe. Fortunately, I had already learned Reiki. I put my new Reiki skill to good use. As soon as the swelling on his head came up, it disappeared. You could tell that Thomas was in quite a bit of pain. The Reiki probably intensified the pain, then relieved it. I note that this was my experience. It may not be the way others perceived the experience. This is important to note: even though we are all having a similar experience, our perception or perspective of that same experience is different.

Around this time, I heard about an amazing cranial-sacral osteopath. Unfortunately, he was in Brisbane for several months so I put Thomas's and my name on his waitlist so we could see him upon his return. Not being one to sit still and wait at this time, we did visit a few other cranial-sacral therapists but none like this therapist. Thomas and I were still visiting him until he took a well-deserved extended break earlier last year.

One of the first things I said to him on our first visit was, "Can I trust you with my son?" He just looked at me and smiled. I am not sure I knew what that smile meant but I sensed he knew what he was doing. I was starting to trust myself, trust what I was feeling.

As Thomas and I explored the natural, alternative therapies, my busyness continued. I was not sitting still. I was not breathing out until yoga entered my life. I would attend a yoga class once a week. My then sister-in-law, Trish, and her friend would baby-sit Thomas for me. It was fantastic. Some "me" time. My body was starting to get some well-needed movement and stretching. Also, I believe it was a wonderful time for Trish to bond with Thomas even though it may not have been easy for her. To this day, I still find yoga to be so important in my daily routine. When I am in Auckland, I enjoy going to a yoga studio that offers restorative yoga. I find this so very beneficial for me. Generally, the Monday class sets me up so well for the week ahead. Otherwise, I do enjoy my short daily yoga class in the comfort of my own home.

What other therapies did I find useful?

RETAIL THERAPY - IS IT THERAPY?

I have written about the alternative, natural therapies I have explored with Thomas on our journey. These therapies have truly supported us to land where we are today. This is true for retail therapy too.

You may laugh, but retail therapy was part of my therapy. I purchased so many toys, teaching aids, and equipment to assist Thomas. Thomas's dad and I spent thousands and thousands of dollars on toys and teaching aids. The spending really affected our liquidity, but I didn't want to worry about it. In my reality, if I didn't worry about it, the problem didn't exist. I was living in the fantasy land and crusade of fixing my son.

At the moment of purchase, the item purchased was going to assist Thomas to get better, be better, fix him, and assist him to become the "normal" boy I wanted him to be. Some of the items purchased were invaluable at the time, but others were not. I spent so much on the equipment, teaching aids, and toys that Thomas had a separate room filled with them.

As time went on, I could see how the retail therapy was a way of avoiding my pain, grief, and fear. My ultimate realisation was that the feel-good factor from purchasing a new toy or item is short-lived, then my reality would return and hit home. Obviously, it was different for a piece of equipment that Thomas truly needed.

It was then that I was able to start giving away some of the items to preschools, therapists, and to other children who would benefit from them.

One thing I know for sure, I will continue to offer different experiences and opportunities to Thomas. This is true for me, too. My adventurous soul needs to be fed.

THE LAND OF OPPORTUNITY, SO I THOUGHT

My first Hong Kong experience was when I was around 20 years old. Such a vibrant, fun, happening, world-class city. This was helped by the fact I was staying with my then-boyfriend's family home in Mt. Nicholson. Those of you who know Hong Kong will know it as a lovely expat area not too far from the central business district and near some wonderful nature walks. It was an ideal spot to make the most of all the great things Hong Kong had to offer. This visit had aroused my curiosity about Asia as had the three weeks' holiday in Singapore, Malaysia, and Thailand just prior. The normal Overseas Experience (OE) was to visit United Kingdom and Europe ... to reconnect with our ancestors and to experience life in the big wide world. Maybe my OE would be to Asia. It was my then-boyfriend's intention to return to Hong Kong to work, and then I was to follow.

Once I completed my bachelor's degree, had a year or so work experience in Wellington, I packed up and headed for Hong Kong. Yes, I followed my boyfriend to the greener pastures of Hong Kong. The pastures weren't so green. I worked my butt off. I was lucky if I got a day off each week. If I had the day off, I made sure I was in nature. I felt I was too exhausted to hike but I made sure I hung out in some sunshine and nature. My treat, at that time was a McDonald's hot-cakes breakfast. So, my Sunday ritual was to sit there for a few hours writing my weekly letters and post cards to friends and family back home. Due to the long work hours, I found it difficult to connect with other people to create friendships. Some of the people I met were called FILTH … Failed In London Try Hong Kong. The naïve, innocent part of me always felt quite threatened and unworthy to be in their company as they seemed to be completely arrogant to me. In those times, I had no idea what I was really feeling, let-alone how to cope with those feelings and emotions.

My job was auditing financial institutions. There was so much work. It seemed like my job was never done. Also, I was taking time to immerse into the Hong Kong way …the locals tended to start work late. The late start, late finish, just didn't gel with my lark personality. I preferred to be in bed early and up early. So, in reverting to my more natural ways, I started to rub my colleagues the wrong way. I guess they thought, *Why is she leaving early?* They hadn't seen me arrive early. Until all the second years at the accounting firm (I was one of them), had a training course and I blitzed them all. They now could see I was doing well. I actually knew my stuff. Finally, there was a level of acceptance, and acknowledgment that their way was not the only way. The associates and partners even acknowledged this. It was a big deal, but this acknowledgement came too late as I had decided to join my boyfriend in Jakarta, Indonesia where a lot more of life was to be experienced.

I had come to Hong Kong, a naïve young New Zealander who really had no experience with many different cultures and lived quite a sheltered upbringing. I was now leaving Hong Kong with some insights into the Chinese culture and customs, sensing they would play a big part in the evolution of world commerce. At that moment, I didn't think I would ever be back to live in Hong Kong. Yet that was exactly what happened after six years in Jakarta, Indonesia. There was more of life to be experienced in Hong Kong.

THANK YOU, HONG KONG

I have spent hours, days, weeks, months, and years exploring the inner workings of me, my patterns, my strategies, my ways of showing up in life or not showing up in life, all my emotions and emotional blocks that kept me from being and delivering my gifts, my unique gifts, to the world.

I have always been truly grateful to Hong Kong for its transformational energy that allowed me to discover so much of my inner world. So much of that inner world had not been explored; it was buried and hidden, and I probably was hoping I never had to look at it. So much of this hidden hurt, pain, and trauma I had absolutely no idea about. The inner wounds of my being. Deep wounds that needed to be discovered, explored, nurtured, and felt, to allow the gift within the wound to be given light, moving to the surface. I encouraged and nourished my wounds to allow the sharing that is happening now.

Thank you, Hong Kong, for the transformational energy to allow my growth. You supported me through numerous life challenges such as the passing of my mum, my divorce from Thomas's dad, Bill and coming to terms with Thomas's numerous health challenges.

MUM IS FINALLY AT PEACE

As I write, I feel the tears well up in me. At my writing desk, I have an altar with objects and photos of people. I have two photos there. One of Thomas. One of my mum. As much as mum taught me how to be, she taught me how not to be.

One of her daily parting words were, "Remember what your name is", her way of saying "Be your best self" which is what I say to my stepson Greg. Oops, I will get in trouble as Greg wants me to call him my son. This isn't to disrespect his mum, Karen. Greg often says he has a heavenly mum and an earthly mum. Greg, you bring a smile not only to my face but my heart.

I missed saying goodbye to Mum in person and I am thankful that the last words I spoke to her on the telephone were, "I love you." She passed away a few hours later that day.

I missed that final hug with her on the day she passed. I hadn't seen her in about three months, but there was blessing a few days after her passing away. While Thomas and I were at her coffin side at the funeral home, her spirit hugged me through Thomas. I knew it was her as the hug was so different from a Thomas hug. Thomas gives me short intense hugs. This hug was a long, lingering motherly hug.

I missed not being at her side when she passed away yet my dad and sisters who lived close weren't there, either. Dad hadn't long left the hospital, only to get a telephone call saying Mum had passed away.

My mum worked hard. Much of her 69 years were spent working hard whether it was raising three daughters or her retail businesses with my dad. She had Addison's Disease for more than 35 years, relying on steroids for her energy. She was able to self-regulate her steroid intake which was fortunate. In stressful situations, mum would increase her steroids, otherwise her health would deteriorate quickly.

Even in the grief and sadness of mum not being physically here, I still feel her presence, her words even in some of the words I say, or others say, and other sounds which were so "mum." I know she was tired. She had done so much for all of us, it was her time to rest, and death was how rest and peace would come to her. So Mum, thank you for being you and for all the encouragement you blessed me with. And for showing me how to be and how not to be.

I think of my mum often. I know she is always with me. I know Thomas can feel you, too, Mum. He really feels you. I am so blessed to have him show me how to have a deeper, greater connection to what is in this moment. There are no words to truly be able to express this.

I miss you, Mum. I still feel short-changed by your passing at 69, yet I know I wouldn't be where I am without your passing on. It was your time. You were exhausted and ready for your peace. I can't believe what you did, to hold things down; everything was held so tight. To keep everything buried so deeply. I am guessing no one knows about the trauma you endured. I am sure the pain, the energy it took to keep your trauma down, was the cause of your cancer. The cancer of the kidney, the Addison disease. When I look at Louise Hay's book, *You Can Heal Your Life*, it states:

Addison's Disease see: Adrenal problems.

Probable Cause: Severe emotional malnutrition. Anger at the self.

New Thought Pattern: I lovingly take care of my body, my mind, and my emotions.

Adrenal Problems:

Probable Cause: Defeatism. No longer caring for the self. Anxiety.

New Thought Pattern: I love and approve of myself. It is safe for me to care for myself.

Cancer:

Probable Cause: Deep hurt. Longstanding resentment. Deep secret or grief eating away at the self. Carrying hatreds. "What's the use?"
New Thought Pattern: I lovingly forgive and release all of the past. I choose to fill my world with joy. I love and approve of myself.

Mum, I can feel, I can sense that you spent a lot of time and energy keeping your trauma down. So very deep down into your cells. It's taken so much energy. I can't imagine how that was possible for so long. I am pleased you got to meet Thomas. I know you struggled with the amount of time I dedicated to him and wanted me to think about me and my own purpose in life. I know you thought I totally lost myself with caring for Thomas and in truth, I did. The truth was the trauma of Thomas's illness and subsequent challenges, and struggle has brought me back to me … my purpose in life.

I didn't know how, when, what, and why to do anything. I lost myself into the world of shock.

The world I didn't recognise. I was lost, with no guidebooks, nothing. I searched for books to assist, books to give me hope, books from other parents who could give me hope, books of truth.

I wanted truth, hope, and promise. Promise that all would be okay. All would be revealed. It was something nobody could give me. I wanted it so badly.

This is why I am here to share my story. To talk about the shock of meningitis, the shocking impact on Thomas, the shocking impact on Thomas's dad and my marriage, the shocking impact on all who knew Thomas. There was quite a ripple effect from this one event.

Only now am I seeing the shock I was in. I was numb to it all. I don't actually remember much of the time except experiences that shocked my mind and body to my soul.

It was the shock of diagnosis. It was shock that something is deemed wrong, not right, different than normal with my once perfect baby boy, Thomas.

So many questions swirled around in my mind. They were on a repeat button as they just didn't stop.

How?

How did he get it?

How was it allowed to happen?

Why?

Why to me?

Why to him?

Why to us?

What next?

What can I really do with a sick baby?

What else can I expect?

Where from here?

When will I get my young baby back?

All the questions and more that came flooding in. No one could answer the questions. It felt so unsatisfactory to me, for me and for Thomas.

What was I to learn from this experience and other life-alternating experiences?

THE ANGEL IN DIVORCE

How much have you heard time is a wonderful healer? My divorce is proof of this.

I now see Thomas's dad, Bill as an angel who has helped and shaped me. He has helped shape me into the woman I am today. It was when my marriage started to collapse that I found The Journey. This was a lifeline back to remembering who I really was. It helped me address the all-important question, "Who are you?"

The experiences with life, the experiences Bill shared with me – and didn't share – have definitely shaped the woman I am today. He has assisted me in finding forgiveness. I must admit there weren't as many "The Journey" (more information below) processes that included him as I thought there may have been. My life path had been planned or mapped out long before I met him.

A lot of my journey processes were with myself, God, and my family. Not that my family did anything wrong, it was a perception the younger me had. The younger me who needed to be heard. My perspective as a young child may have been different from what was intended or the actual reality of what happened but the younger me needed to be heard and seen and forgiven.

"The Journey" process is a transformational technique in which I am trained. We worked in pairs and would facilitate and witness each other through a lot of the repressed emotions. For me, feeling the repressed emotions was initially challenging, but over time, these processes became integral to my way of living life fully expressed.

I connected a lot with the younger me, realising she had kept quiet so very often. She didn't want to be seen and heard at that time. Yet it is exactly what I want to be now … the paradox of life. A childhood of being quiet and just getting on with it and now in adulthood, I want to share, talk, speak, and teach. Teach others to share, too. It's about teaching others to stand up and be counted in whatever they are choosing to do. This is the time to share from the vulnerability, from the unknown of what it is. It was good. It was truth. It was all that was required.

The divorce taught me to stand on my own two feet. Taught me to stand tall, (all 5 foot 3 and half inches of me), standing with an aligned back. Accept what had happened. Respect what had happened. Love what had happened. It was beautiful, really.

LETTER TO THOMAS'S DAD

Dear Bill,

Now I am so thankful for what you have taught me … what you continue to teach me …

Thomas is a gift who just keeps giving.

I celebrate him so very much. He is teaching me and has taught me so much. He is a master of the highest order, an amazing human being, amazing spirit and soul.

At times, I can't believe Thomas chose me to be his parent. I am so very honoured to be his student and Mum.

Bill, the lessons from our dating, married, and divorced life are continuing to shape who I am and how I am in my marriage to David. (I know I haven't mentioned David before. On 20th November 2013, he, along with his three children entered Thomas's and my life, bringing us much love, joy and challenge of creating a new family.) I appreciate the learning, so I won't repeat past perspectives or perceived mistakes. I know there was a co-creation of our divorce.

I know others may view our divorce differently. In divorce much healing has happened. It created an opening for healing from childhood traumas endured, way before we met.

People say you are happy now, married and happy. I am so pleased for you. I hope you, like me, have learned from our marriage and time together so that the same challenges are not repeated. I can't believe I am writing this. It's hard to imagine this being published and yet the reader needs to know there is light after divorce. There is huge learning and a way to move forward with forgiveness and gratitude.

I am totally thankful for the learning from you, our marriage and our divorce.

With compassion and acceptance,
Nicky

Note to readers: I didn't always feel this way. I feel such a relief to allow the blame, shame, and judgement related to the divorce to go. Such freedom in letting it go. But....

THE OTHER SIDE OF THE LETTER

The dark nights of divorce were so painful. The fights, the pushing (not physically), the pulling, the upset, the anger and rage, the pushing Bill out, the talking to him like a teenager – or was it a toddler. Yes, it felt like I had two children: Bill and Thomas.

It took time to want to look at what was holding me back from the life I had dreamed. It was time to face the facts, face the truth and be done with the childhood trauma that was holding me back. At the time, I couldn't believe we weren't to experience this together. I guess it was about fear. I guess it was about my own divine timing.

I know when it comes to facing fear that the fear can be sometimes so overwhelming. It is too great, too intense, and I have turned away from it instead of facing it, feeling it, and walking through it.

It feels like there is some resolution around all my life traumas, just like everyone else.

In those dark days prior to making a decision to get divorced, I made up stories to friends. I lied to them about so many different aspects of my life. I felt shame that I wasn't able to make my marriage work. The internal picture was not a mirror for the veneer I was trying to portray. I wasn't doing this with the intention to deceive. I thought I was protecting what I knew it to be, the illusion of a perfect family.

I remember Bill missing the photo shoot with Thomas and me. I was totally amazed at how well the photos came out. It was as if Thomas and I were totally in the joy of that moment. We were able to put aside whatever was happening in our life and be in the moment of the photo shoot. I used to associate this photo shoot with all the things that didn't happen, remembering who wasn't present. This was totally unusual for me as I consider myself to be a half-full kinda girl.

Now when I look the photos from this photo shoot, although there is a slight backstory which enters my mind, I really see the beautiful photos of Thomas and me mirroring the pure joy, love, and connection with what was there in that moment. I am so pleased we were able to be in that place at that time. Upon reflection this is evidence of me being able to live in the moment and be present to the moment. The photos are a reflection of what was there, that's for sure. Being truly present to who I was and who Thomas was in that moment. This experience showed Thomas and I a way, a way we could show up in joy despite all the life challenges we had. We were going to move forward with life. With or without Bill. It was Thomas's and my choice to move forward, learn, and evolve, to be the next best version of ourselves. I use the word, "our" intentionally here as I believe Thomas was part of this decision. I believe Thomas wanted to move forward, learn, evolve his spirituality, his reason for being here as much I did. In truth, he was further along that path of self-actualisation than I was. I didn't see this at the time. I could only see it in hindsight as time and I had moved forward, and I had allowed myself time to reflect. Hindsight is such a wonderful gift when you use the wisdom from it to move an inspired step forward, learning from the past challenges.

Fortunately, the divorce happened quickly, allowing us both the freedom to move forward. In truth, I was probably expressing that freedom well before the confirmed Decree Absolute date.

It was when Bill had moved out of our apartment to his own apartment that I felt free to start to explore a part of me that was hidden deep within me. I enjoyed the freedom. I enjoyed the party. I enjoyed the sense of something new yet there were past traumas and challenges to meet. I probably didn't meet these challenges in the traditional ways. These were the ways I am ashamed of and deeply embarrassed, and I am owning them. They were experiences I had. The encounters I had over a six-month period helped me define who I was and who I was not. There were a few lovely men who assisted me with this learning and healing. Fortunately, it only took those six short months to realise what was happening, what had happened, and there was no need to continue in this vein.

The healing I needed to do next was the healing of my past traumas. I needed to give myself space, time to do what was needed to allow this healing and in a place that would be truly nurturing and nourishing to my soul.

WHERE TO LIVE?

For some time, I had the sense I was going to take Thomas back to New Zealand. And yet I knew I wanted to stay in Hong Kong as I had made an assumption that I wouldn't find a man in New Zealand. Now I smile internally and externally at this assumption. This turned out to be so wrong and it was an assumption and belief that had a tight grip on my psyche.

Aside from the assumption I would not find a man in New Zealand, I also wanted Thomas to deepen his relationship with his dad. It wasn't my primary reason but nevertheless, I am so grateful that Thomas and I did remain in Hong Kong for several years after Thomas's dad and I divorced. They have a lovely relationship.

Hong Kong offered Thomas and me the option of Thomas being totally supported by caregivers or as we called them in Hong Kong, helpers. The helpers Thomas had were generally extremely qualified people, physios, nurses, and teachers who decided to work abroad, as the Hong Kong salary was better than their home country. They not only were skilled at their particular profession, but they were kind-hearted people. Having the support of helpers allowed me the freedom to explore whatever I needed to explore.

That said, in 2012 Thomas made it clear that we needed to leave Hong Kong and return to my home country of New

Zealand when he had a seizure and stopped breathing. In that moment, I knew it was time to stop procrastinating and move back to New Zealand. New Zealand was home to me, and Thomas and I had the support of family there. I yearned the fresh air, open spaces and to be closer to family. But where in New Zealand? I looked at all the options within the North and South Island. I even considered Australia. Once all the pros and cons were listed and considered, my decision was Auckland. The main reason for Auckland was the Starship Children's Hospital. Obviously, I knew Thomas would grow up. I hoped the Auckland Hospital would be just as good for him as an adult.

So, Auckland it was. It was Auckland City, not any of the outlying islands which may have been good for me but not necessarily as good for Thomas.

In hindsight, I can, hand on heart, totally say it was a great decision not to be on one of the outlying islands as there have been many ambulance rides, Accident & Emergency visits and hospital stays.

STAY OR NOT STAY/LIVE OR DIE

In 1998, Thomas wasn't expected to survive the pneumococcal meningitis. Only 4% of those who contract it do survive, but normally with numerous lifelong challenges. It was a few days after his initial admission to Queen Mary Hospital in Hong Kong that I found out that the doctors' thought Thomas wasn't going to survive. It wasn't that the doctor told us this. It was because we were given special access to this small side room off the main ICU ward.

Thomas had been in ICU for a day or so, and we assumed we could still use the room the following day as we had the day before, but we weren't allowed in. The doctors and nurses wouldn't tell us why at the time. I just thought it's another dumb hospital rule. It was after witnessing the use of "that room" over a few days and weeks that followed, I knew the purpose of "that room." It was for grieving parents and families whose young babies in ICU were in the process of passing away. It is still heart wrenching to think of "that room." Some years later, I even met a family who remember "that room." We even spoke about "that room." Unfortunately, their young son passed away from the very same meningitis Thomas had. This family has touched my life, and indeed Thomas's life, forever.

I don't really know why Thomas survived that initial brush with death and why he has survived all his other brushes with death, other than it's his soul-choice. All I can say is there is something within him that is keeping him alive. There is a reason. There is a purpose to be revealed.

Thomas's physical body has been compromised from the meningitis. His left side is paralysed, he has an injured brain, he has bilaterally profound deafness, and he has epilepsy. These are constant challenges for him and everyone who knows him.

I sometimes find it difficult to understand why he just didn't give up on life. As I mentioned there have been numerous times when it seemed like Thomas was making a choice. A choice of whether to stay or whether to go. To live or to die.

I remember when he was acutely ill with the meningitis. A dear friend gave me a prayer from her mother. I prayed the prayer over Thomas. The full prayer is included in my first book, *Trust Life's Journey* should you want to find it. Although I found it extremely difficult to say the prayer over Thomas and truly mean it, there was an element of peace within me that arose from saying this prayer.

In each of these "choice" moments, I observed there was a different level of surrender by those near and dear to Thomas. It was up to them to explore that within themselves. My sense was that Thomas continued to be who he was in that moment and each and every moment thereafter.

For me, each brush with death, brought new insight, a new way of being ever more present to what life was about. It seemed to allow me to express more freely without judgment, without fear, without rage. The words came from a place of love, unconditional love, not only for Thomas, but for family, my new family and beyond. Note that when I speak of family, family includes friends who have walked very closely along this journey with Thomas and me.

ANOTHER INCIDENT LEADS TO SURGERY

Thomas was at Queen Mary Hospital again. In Hong Kong, Queen Mary Hospital was our local hospital so given Thomas's medical challenges I was so pleased that it wasn't far from where we lived.

Thomas had been having violent seizures. This particular evening, he fell in his bathroom while getting into his bath. The seizure stopped and we were able to settle him as we always did. But we were not prepared for what we were greeted with the following morning. Thomas was not looking like Thomas. His face appeared to be fill of fluid. He looked bloated. What? ... How could this be?

Out came the doer, super mum. I needed to know what was happening. I needed to get the tests, scans done so I knew. You wouldn't believe how long it took to arrange a scan. I was totally stressed about it as any parent would be. I wasn't sure why the doctors Thomas and I were visiting were not as stressed as I was. I knew he needed a CT scan. I really don't know why they could not see that. Fortunately, not too long after, Thomas had a follow-up appointment with the Neurosurgeon and a CT scan was planned and performed. It showed that Thomas's VP shunt (A ventriculoperitoneal (VP) shunt is a thin plastic tube that is surgically inserted to drain extra cerebrospinal fluid (CSF) from the brain) had been broken ... probably the result of the fall in the bathroom. Thomas's ventricles were now filling compared with the previous CT scan. It appeared his brain was starting to fill with fluid, creating pressure which could end in hydrocephalus.

Then I was asked a question from the Neurosurgeon. "Do we operate?" he asked me.

I looked at him trying not to show my shock, probably not succeeding and said in a very calm voice.

"If we operate sooner, we will not have to deal with an emergency situation. I believe if we wait, it will become an emergency situation."

The Neurosurgeon looked me straight in the eyes then nodded his head, "I believe you are right. We need to operate now." I was shocked again. Prior to this appointment, the doctors' perspectives and my perspective appeared to be at opposite ends of the spectrum. Now something was aligning us.

The surgery was planned.

Along with Thomas's dad, I waited outside the surgery suite. Nerve-racking, to say the least. There was a part of me that didn't know for sure the surgery was the right thing to do but I knew the surgeon had agreed with me and I felt better that we were on the same page. Finally, I felt that the doctors and I were working well together.

After a few Starbuck coffees (the only coffee shop available at the hospital so it was definitely better than nothing) Thomas's surgery was over. It had been two hours. I was so grateful that the Neurosurgeon came to see us as soon as the surgery was completed to report firstly, Thomas was doing well, and secondly, we had made the right decision to operate today as the pressure had started to build on Thomas's brain. If they had delayed, there would have been a real emergency situation.

The Neurosurgeon had listened. He had acted on my feelings and Thomas's life was spared again. And again, it happens...

ARE THE PEARLY GATES CALLING?

Late 2012, Thomas and I moved back to Auckland, New Zealand. The reason I say back to, was that prior to 2012, Thomas and I used to stay in Auckland for several months a year to visit doctors, attend therapies, and the Hearing House School preschool. It had always felt like a second home as we had roots there, with dear friends, and some family.

While back in Auckland, there were a number of incidents where I believe Thomas was at the pearly gates, making a decision to go or stay or perhaps being told it wasn't his time now.

It was a day that Thomas was having his teeth checked ... even though we had regularly taken Thomas to the dentist for check-ups he rarely opened his mouth for the dentist. Sometimes if they were lucky, they may have gotten a look inside his mouth, but generally Thomas's mouth was a no-go zone. His mouth was zip-locked shut. So as an extreme precaution, we decided to put him under general anaesthesia so the dentist could have an unencumbered look at Thomas's teeth and general oral hygiene. Fortunately, the condition of his teeth wasn't as bad as we thought. The clean healthy diet was paying off.

Thomas was under general anaesthesia for an oral exam once before in Hong Kong ... the investigation and time under general anaesthesia had gone well but it was the coming out of general anaesthesia that created a problem for him and those of us caring for him. He became aggressive. We wanted him to rest in his hospital bed to allow the general anaesthesia time to wear off. But in true Thomas fashion, he had a completely different plan. Thomas wanted to move anywhere and everywhere in the hospital ward even though his legs weren't really awake to take him. Talk about a strong will, talk about sheer determination to get moving. This experience was ingrained in my memory, so I did not want a repeat of it.

So, we planned the oral examination under general anaesthesia. All the doctors were informed of the previous challenges. I felt I had done my work as a super mum.

All went well during the general anaesthesia … oral examination as well as some hearing tests.

BUT….

In recovery, Thomas started to vomit. And it didn't seem to stop, so the first anti-nausea medication was given.

I was questioned many times whether I had given Thomas food. I quickly became frustrated about this. I knew it was nil by mouth prior to general anaesthesia. I had asked two of Thomas's caregivers to work that very day so they could keep Thomas distracted from food. Obviously, the nurses and doctors couldn't make sense of this, so it felt like they were wanting to blame someone … me. I wasn't having it. A red rash started on my neck and face (a sign of my emotions rising. I could feel my blood pumping, my heart beating louder and louder).

As the vomiting wasn't stopping, the second dose of anti-nausea medication was given. The vomiting started to slow but Thomas clearly wasn't recovering as he should.

This was obviously something they were not ready for as Greenlane Hospital was a day-stay hospital. An ambulance was being arranged to transfer Thomas to a general hospital,

Starship Children's Hospital. I remember the conversation about which hospital to go to. Even though Thomas was on the verge of becoming an adult, Starship Children's Hospital felt more appropriate.

We faced this dilemma every time we were in the ambulance; Starship Children's Hospital versus Auckland's adult hospital. Although there was a protocol, an adult hospital wasn't appropriate for a young person with a disability. I would dearly love to see a hospital that caters for this group of young people who have adult bodies but being in an adult ward isn't appropriate for them or the others in the ward.

Thomas and I arrived at the Accident & Emergency (A & E) of Starship Children's Hospital. We went straight to the resuscitation area. The two caregivers who had been on duty to assist me with Thomas met me there. They must have wondered what they had stepped into. I was puzzled, and I was sure they were, too. I didn't know what was going on. The doctors were not talking to me. Then the "warrior mum" appeared.

"What is going on with Thomas?" I demanded.

No one really answered me.

There was so much busyness in my mind and in the room. I was in shock. What was happening? What was happening to my son?

When the chief doctor arrived, I assumed she was the head of the A & E. She said Thomas wasn't being responsive. They needed to work out what was going on.

She wanted to get a pain response from him. She forcefully pushed on his chest, and I could see Thomas react.

In that moment, they knew.

In that moment, I knew. I knew Thomas had chosen to stay a bit longer. Thomas woke around 11 p.m., a good eight hours after his general anaesthesia. It was time to walk the corridors of the A & E, then have a quick drink before falling back into bed. Thomas and I slept the remainder of the night in a side room in the A & E. Fortunately, due to the previous experience with general anaesthesia, the hospital had allocated a helper to Thomas in case of him becoming aggressive. I wouldn't be able to cope with his behaviour by myself.

This wasn't to be the last incident.

THE BLACK HOLE

Yet again it was another hospital visit, more precisely a visit to Starship Children's Hospital A & E. Thomas had not been well, mainly vomiting. Thomas had had a recent visit to his neurologist at Auckland Hospital ... we had noticed his stability on his feet wasn't good so the appointment with the neurologist was timely. Believe it or not, Thomas vomited while in the doctor's consulting room. This meant he had a five-hour nap in the back-consultation rooms. The conclusion from blood tests were that he was toxic ... his level of Tegretol – an anti-seizure medication taken by Thomas daily - was too high so his daily medication levels needed to be adjusted. Over the next few days his balance improved but not the vomiting. Thus, we were in Starship Children's Hospital A & E again.

I had toyed with the idea of taking him to the local White Cross clinic but decided, rightly, that Starship Children's Hospital was the best option for Thomas. I let my partner know where we were so he could come to support me.

As Thomas and I arrived at the reception of A & E, Thomas promptly vomited. Thomas received immediate attention, skipping the queue. Thomas always knows how to get the attention he needs. He has a natural way of managing to get to the front of any queue. Normally, he uses his charm and killer smile. Shall we call it a gift? On this day I was thankful for this gift.

The usual junior nurses and doctor checks were carried out in Thomas's cubicle. On the surface everything seemed okay. I reminded them that he had been vomiting, and not stable on his feet. Something was not right. I suggested a CT scan, knowing that Thomas may need general anaesthesia during it. General anaesthesia wasn't a very palatable choice but was the only way we could find out what was happening in his brain.

Dr. Emma entered Thomas's cubicle to discuss the options. I suspected she wanted to send us on our way. Clinically, Thomas was fine. All the visual and normal checks didn't indicate anything major was going on except … I had a sense. I suspected she sensed the same.

Then Thomas had a seizure. I moved over to where he was lying on the hospital bed.

"Thomas, are you okay? I am here with you," I said as he was seizing.

At this time Dr Emma joined me at the side of Thomas's bed.

Then it happened.

As I was looking into Thomas's eyes, all I could see was a black hole … a hole of nothingness. No one, nobody was there. There was a stark contrast to how Thomas's eyes normally looked when I peered into Thomas's eyes. I had always seen so much life, a brightness, the touch of innocence, vast wisdom and knowingness. But in this moment, there was nothing.

"Thomas, Thomas. I am here."

Dr Emma was there. She saw what I saw. Nothing.

Was this going to be Thomas's moment to depart this world?

We both silently acknowledged what had just happened.

Then Thomas started to breathe again and something, someone, had returned to his eyes.

I took a breath, as I had been holding my breath. I couldn't move but I needed to sit. Dr Emma helped me back to the chair placed on the other wall.

"You saw that didn't you?"

"Yes," she said.

Tears welled.

Then they streamed down my face, gathering at the tips of my chin and nose. *Where are those tissues when you need them?* I thought. Dr. Emma departed. She now knew what needed to be done. A CT scan was given top priority.

In the meantime, I telephoned Thomas's dad, Bill, to inform him of the situation. Fortunately, he was able to get a flight from Hong Kong within a day or so, so he was able to be there to support Thomas.

What the CT scan showed was that Thomas's VP shunt (A ventriculoperitoneal shunt is a thin plastic tube that helps drain extra cerebrospinal fluid (CSF) from the brain) needed to be replaced. So, the surgery was scheduled and performed in the following few days. All went well. The only problem was that the neurosurgeon had to leave part of the old shunt in his brain as it may have caused more problems trying to remove it. So, the best decision was to leave that piece in-situ.

Thomas continues to grace us with his presence. I often pray a quiet prayer to myself. Please may this shunt last longer than the previous one.

CAN YOU TRUST THEM?

Prior to Thomas contracting pneumococcal meningitis, I thought doctors knew what to do in each and every situation. For some reason, I had them standing up there on the pedestal, up there with God. Doctors just knew what to do, all the time.

Why do we as a society put them there? I don't know and I don't want to explore or even think about it further than I have.

Why don't we want to take control of our own life and trust our own inner wisdom and intuition? I really don't know.

I guess one reason is that we are conditioned by the generations that have gone before us. Thus, we are not in tune with ourselves, our bodies, our emotions, our beliefs, and our purpose in life.

In 1998, there were about five doctors over a period of 30 hours, who made decisions that I wholeheartedly accepted, which led me to taking control of not only my health and wellness but the health and wellness of my son Thomas.

And in those 30 hours, Thomas moved from being a bubbly, standing, 9 ½-month-old, filled with all the joys of life to an impotent, critically ill baby lying in Queen Mary Hospital ICU, fighting for his life. I was there in shock. I wasn't able to be at his side much due to the rules of ICU. I really was numb with shock.

I lost all confidence in doctors. Even though a few had acted with intention and under a guiding light of God, the others appeared to be the total opposite. It was time to take control of Thomas's health – and mine. It was time to get a handle on all of Thomas's illness and become a full advocate for health and wellness in both of our lives.

Today, we have a Wellness Plan for Thomas. It's about keeping his body in the best possible condition, so he is able to do what he wants. Wellness is the focus. I would like to say we have prevented illness, but we haven't. What we have done is give Thomas a far better chance at living a full life and meeting his potential by attending to his well-being … and my wellness, too.

I do remember using the words, "I am into preventative medicine," thinking I could prevent anything bad, any disease from happening. You see, I was under the illusion that I could control it all. Fortunately, my mind has allowed my illusion of control to soften and let go of that knowing. Life is life. Life has challenges, it's the way it is. The important thing is the way we respond to the challenges. I smile to myself inwardly and outwardly. There is such bliss in letting go.

I wondered how I ever thought I could have prevented any of this happening. I feel Thomas smiling, too. I feel his presence even though he is asleep in Auckland, New Zealand, and I am in Jacksonville, Florida, USA.

Now I trust my gut, my intuition. It guides me in each and every moment. Sometimes my gut is aligned with the doctors and sometimes it isn't. I am not afraid to speak, share, and advocate for Thomas. In times where I am unable to, I trust like-spirited friends to guide me.

PARALYSING FEAR – ANOTHER WAKE-UP CALL

Hong Kong is a city full of vibrancy, colour, smells, the sights stimulating all your senses ... it can be a total sensory overload. You really need to stand here and absorb it all, breathe it in and remember to breathe out.

I had been living there for a number of years. One of my favourite events was the Hong Kong sevens ... If you Google Hong Kong, one of the top things to do is to attend the Hong Kong Sevens weekend ... a seven aside rugby tournament played at a great pace, resulting in a winning team at the end of a two-and-a-half-day weekend. It is a serious party with people wearing costumes of anything imaginable. Did I mention a lot of alcohol? Yes, it's definitely party time.

Anyway, my friend and I were there but had decided not to be drinking this weekend. We were loving the rugby, the general fun, and the party atmosphere. I felt I was in my element.

At the end of the evening, there was always a crowd crush exiting the 40,000-capacity Hong Kong stadium. Once through the crush, we decided to take a tram to central Hong Kong, then transit to where we lived.

We sat ourselves on the top level, as the tram has two levels, just to take in the night lights of Hong Kong ... always so bright. We were enjoying the scene the lights create. My mind wondered what was happening behind the lights … The night was a little humid, but the movement of the tram created a welcomed breeze.

As we settled in our seats, we started to have a meaningful conversation about life … then I started to feel a bit off, a bit nauseated, so I moved to the front of the tram so I could see where we were going (this always helped me if I was feeling motion sickness). I managed to walk down part of the stairs, as the tram was stopping, only to find myself lying on the concrete in a park in Statute Square in Central, Hong Kong.

How did I get there?

Well, according to my friend, I collapsed through the front doors of the tram, off the tram just as it was stopping … fortunately there weren't any taxis and buses zooming by at that moment.

I don't know how long I was out.

What I did know was that when I regained consciousness, I couldn't move my arms and legs. I was paralysed. My mind wasn't. It was buzzing, mainly with fear.

My friend had called an ambulance. The paramedics carried out their standard checks. Everything was normal.

What they knew was, I had to go to hospital….

My friend accompanied me in the ambulance, arriving at Queen Mary Hospital Accident and Emergency, which wasn't too far away. Queen Mary Hospital was a hospital I knew far too well. This was the hospital Thomas had visited so often.

It wasn't long before the doctors and nurses were doing all the routine checks. I could tell they were totally perplexed by the fact I couldn't use my arms and legs, as was I.

I realised I was paralysed by fear. I couldn't deny the fear I had as I fell out of the tram. I had to feel my fear to get out of that hospital bed.

Fortunately, my friend was wise enough to connect with me. She was a coach of sorts, and sat with me and took me through a process, allowing me to feel my fear. During this process I realized that the fear I was feeling was the fear not only from falling out of the tram but the fear I had repressed when I collapsed onto the floor of the Adventist Hospital nine years earlier when I feared Thomas would die of pneumococcal meningitis. My friend guided me, so the fear wouldn't overrun, or overtake me and put me in a worse situation than I was already in.

As I felt the fear, I felt the release and my body started to move.

Nothing the doctors did helped me to move again. In fact, they were shocked when I walked out of the hospital later that evening.

I found it so amazing that this was the exact hospital Thomas was driven to by ambulance when he was critically ill with pneumococcal meningitis; where he stayed for several weeks. I was so fearful that Thomas would die.

This was a significant event in my life of realising the impact of my repressed emotions. It was another wake-up call, because it allowed me to re-evaluate my life and start making conscious decisions toward having the life I truly desired. I had a heartfelt desire to assist other parents of loved ones with lifelong challenges, support them, stop their worry and overwhelmingly empower them to see these challenges as priceless gifts.

What other fears had I suppressed? I started my inquiry … my internal inquiry.

FEAR OF FLYING

I am an adventurous soul ... I enjoy the adventure. This was really ignited on my first trip abroad from New Zealand at the age of 20. There was excitement about travelling and having new adventures. With the beauty of hindsight, I now see that all the adventures were definitely a way to keep me moving, avoiding some deeply hidden emotions.

I really don't remember when the discomfort of flying started but I know I felt it for years. When I allowed myself the time to explore my feelings and emotions, I realised I had a fear of flying. I did not acknowledge my fear of flying because I was so detached from it. I even would laugh at my mum when she talked about it. Generally, this was after something had happened to her on a flight. My inward laugh was a nervous laugh, because in truth, I was exactly like her.

I have had a number of experiences on flights when I have begun to overheat, hadn't taken my warm layers off quickly enough, and have ended up passing out.

I remember one occasion in 2011 when I was flying from Hong Kong to Auckland to attend the 2011 Rugby World Cup. The time leading to my departure had been particularly stressful. Anyway, I had a window seat and could feel myself getting warmer and warmer. I asked the guy seated next to me to move so I could go to the bathroom but before I knew it, I collapsed over a passenger two seats in front. It was a lovely

French man. I smile at the memory. The lengths I went to obtain some male attention!

Fortunately, there was a lovely Irish male doctor on the flight who was able to ensure I was okay. He was able to determine that I just had low blood pressure in that moment. With the doctor's suggestion, I was able to lie in the bulkhead area right by the door with my legs up the wall. This allowed me to regain stability and a normal blood pressure. It had been my intention to drive myself to my hotel, but the crew called my friend, Sandra Feran, to ask her if she was able to pick me up. I was so very thankful she was able to.

I have never admitted that I have had chest pains on a plane every time I flew. I would try to make myself as comfortable as possible, but I always end up feeling like crap. I never admitted this until I mentioned it in a conversation with my husband David recently. I can't believe I teased my mum about being scared of flying. The truth was, I actually was, too.

I had been denying it for ages. Now that I have acknowledged the fear, the chest pains have reduced. It is now that I acknowledge the anxiety that some Rescue Remedy – a natural stress remedy is required and just allow the anxiety to be. Anxiety is here because it is here.

Why I am anxious about flying? I am not sure.

It's okay not to know. It's okay to not know. It's okay to not know. I repeat this to myself. Or I let that thought go into the "I don't know (IDK)" bucket. It's like I am conditioning myself to be in the unknown. The IDK bucket, the mystery bucket of it all. It's okay not to know. Letting go of the why?

There has always been a part of me that has been searching for knowledge, searching for great marks at school, searching and or seeking to understand.

Fortunately, I now recognise my signs of anxiety whether it be my heart racing, my chest pains or discomfort or generally overheating. So, I act. I also centre myself and get myself into my “fit to fly” mode by taking Rescue Remedy, by having layers of clothing so I can easily remove them should I become slightly warm. I travel with more ease and grace these days. Thank you, Mum.

Being an adventurous soul, I had always sought adventures externally. Now I was starting to explore and adventure internally.

MY CONSTANT MOVEMENT HID MY FEAR

In all of my motion, in all of my movement and adventure, I wasn't allowing myself to rest, be still, and just exhale. I wasn't aware of this for many years as I was just so busy being in motion and doing.

As I allowed myself to have fun and allow joy into my life, I noticed I was allowing other emotions to come to the surface. I wasn't always aware of what was I was feeling but I knew it was something, as I was uncomfortable.

It took time to realise it was an underlay of anxiety and fear about everything, about not being good enough, not being worthy, not being loved; and the list goes on.

So, I started to be calmer and enjoy that stillness. And the emotions came flooding.

FEAR'S GRIP ON ME

Fear has had such a hold on me. I feared so many things; people and life. What I was most fearful of was fear itself. Sounds weird but it was true for me.

It was only in August 2018 when I stood on stage to speak my truth, that I truly got it. The terrible headaches and altitude sickness had "befriended" me on this speaker course until I let my body know I was going to speak no matter what. Even when I stood on stage and froze. A frozen mind, heart, and mouth. I could not speak. I stood there in it until the allotted time was over. My fellow participants applauded even though I had frozen. I stood on stage again and again. My body, mind, and soul were becoming more comfortable, yet not comfortable enough.

I began feeling an opening. At times I was so lost in the moment, I couldn't remember the words at all. Then there was a flow of words, but I really don't remember what was said. All I know was it landed with the audience, as many told me afterwards. I had to get out of my mind, out of my head, and speak what came. I needed to move forward from where I was. I needed to take one step forward to the next speech, the next book, the next phase of life.

MY MIND LETS GO

Awakening my impact to the world has been five decades in the making. It has been a long-time coming, releasing and really ready to fully release. In some ways I have been ready for years, but my mind hasn't allowed it. My mind has been buying into a lot of beliefs, statements, and untruths of how I wasn't ready, not good enough, didn't have the qualifications and so the excuses and procrastination continued. I can hear myself going blah, blah, blah. On reflection, I have found it amazing to see how my mind-talk has kept me from being me for ages, for years.

Now there is no stopping me. No stopping. Not even fear. My fear is being faced, felt fully, acknowledged, and defeated. It has allowed all of me to be in this process called life. It has been a process of how I can stand still, sure and strong in my belief that I am ready to defeat it all. It has been a ride to get here … to this place of allowing the ride to take me, knowing the universe has my back. I haven't always trusted that.

All is in my highest and best good, even though I may not understand the significance of it all.

I love my life as it is. I am looking forward to being of service to others who are struggling with the burden of life challenges, sharing with them, or asking inquisitive questions, listening to my inner wisdom, providing the mirror to my clients, being their mirror and witness. So, they can come to a place of peace by finding their joy, wonder, and trust in their own inner wisdom.

I am seeing this. I am witnessing this. It is an honour and pleasure to be a witness and of service.

As we awaken to our own wisdom so does the wisdom of the world awaken.

As we realise our unique gifts, the possibilities of the world are expanded, and the world is a richer place.

This is why I am assisting parents and families who have loved ones with challenges; to assist them with their stumbling blocks, their burnout, worry, and living half a life, so they can find their road to peace and joy and living their fullest lives.

By being at peace, finding the joy in life again, you are in the best possible place to assist your loved one with challenges, finding their purpose and gift.

By looking after you, being purposeful and energised, you then have the energy, the desire to assist your loved ones wholeheartedly. So often you are doing things that don't fulfill you. They decrease your energy so there is no energy, no creative energy to help our loved ones who have challenges.

I am to be in this world to offer all of me to you. All that is here for you.

It hasn't always been this way. I have experienced many of life's challenges to be at this place. This place isn't a destination, it's a spot on the journey called life. There has been lots of colour. At times exciting, at times terrifying, much sadness and happiness – and now there is a lot of joy.

There was joy in my earlier life, but I didn't allow it as much as I do now. I was blocking so many deep emotions that I didn't have the energy, the life force, to allow the ecstasy or the pure joy.

As I let go, more of me was being revealed to me and to the world, and I realised I had been covering up a level of anxiety. Anxiety about so many things such as being anxious about what others might think. I was anxious about whether I was good enough to be doing, thinking, experiencing what is. Now I know joy has become me.

All emotions have flowed through me, I am flooded with all emotions. None are left untouched. Thank you to life for providing the richness of experience so I can be right here in this moment.

WHAT ABOUT ME?

I love the way my son Greg says to me, "Nicky, when are you writing a book about me?"

Greg, finally you have your wish. I am mentioning your name in my book.

Greg had a wonderful insight at the tender age of 10. I think I had just met him. I had known his dad, David, all of a few weeks. Greg was a passenger in my car. I had the roof down, and we were parked in his sister's school waiting for them.

Greg ever so casually says, "Nicky, you know you are going to be my stepmother."

"Am I?" I say in shock.

"Yes, you are," he replies.

"Thank you for sharing this with me, Greg."

The conversation was so matter of the fact. We continued talking about something else, but I was thinking, *How does he know this?* Both David and I were feeling this way and sensed our relationship was going to go the distance. By this I mean marriage. We both knew. We both felt the vulnerability in sharing this with each other.

Even though we had only just met.

Even though David's children were still grieving their mother's passing.

Even though it was going to be a push in trust as to how we would get to know everything about each other, yet there was this knowing and trust in the gut instinct to follow it, to follow the love.

I didn't want to follow my mind. I could hear the inner dialogue: *It's too quick. It's too quick,* I asked myself. *How do I know I am ready? I don't know much about his background.* Yet my heart knew.

With trust, I took a step forward. Then I took the next step not knowing how that step may unfold.

WILL THE TEENAGERS EVER GROW UP?

Greg has been a challenge in the past few years. In the past month, on his most recent visit in 2019 to Florida, I have seen a change in him.

All are beautiful children; each with their own special uniqueness, their wants and dreams.

From giving birth to one child, Thomas; to being the co-guardian with David's three children has been a huge challenge for me. It wasn't something I consciously thought about. I followed my heart and my love for David.

Being a person who always thought things through, I am totally amazed at myself. I hadn't put a lot of thought into the fact that when I agreed to marry David, I was going to help David co-guardian his and Karen's children. I had chosen to put my mind on the back seat. I just sensed that it would be alright. It would all work out.

I also acknowledge that part of me that loves fantasy, that goes straight to the place in my mind we are all going to get on well together. There wasn't another option.

I had projected this scenario on us all without knowing it. There wasn't much conscious thought as to how we would get there. It was challenging for both David and me and no doubt the children. The teenage challenges pushed David and me to discuss many issues. Sometimes David and I disagreed; we were at opposite ends of the spectrum with certain challenges. It was a reflection of our polarity and being two very different human beings. As time does, it allows space for each of us to experience, grow, reflect the beautiful space of unconditional love.

But how did Karen feel about it? I wondered.

ENCOUNTERS WITH KAREN

In the early days of dating David, I could feel the presence of Karen around me. It felt like she was watching my every move. I felt like I was being tested to see if I was up to the task of looking after her beloved family.

There are two particular incidents I vividly remember.

The first was upon my return home in Orakei, Auckland. I had been out in my car. I drove into my garage and as soon as I opened my car door, I can hear someone puffing as if they had been running. It was loud enough to me that I walked behind the car outside the garage, looking to see if someone was looking for me. But I couldn't find a physical person. Then I received this sense it was Karen. So, I spoke to her. I don't recall what was said, that's not important. The important thing was she wanted to let me know she was around, and she was checking me out. Was I going to assist David to look after her babies? Interestingly enough, I asked David if Karen was a runner. You know what? She was!

The second incident was when I was having a healing treatment. The healer and I could both sense Karen's presence. It was at a time when Alicia and Siân were being particularly challenging, just the normal teenage stuff – and of course they were still grieving their mum. I was at a loss as to what to do. It was in that healing I let go of all my should's, my supposed-to's, any ideas of how others deemed I could connect with them and listened to my intuition and guidance. My intuition was saying, *Be me.* Sometimes that meant tough love, sometimes it meant being the "jellyfish" guardian but mostly, it was about unconditional love.

The fascinating thing about it was, as soon as I connected with that realisation within myself, the healer, I could sense Karen's energy leave. I got what she wanted me to understand and implement. Since that day, I haven't felt her presence as intensely.

I am taking from that, that she is at peace with the way I am caring, loving, and accepting her family.

I still feel the sadness of the children, even though they are now young adults. I feel sad they have had to go through losing their mum at such an early age. And in that sadness, I know that is where joy is, and stillness is.

THE ROLLER-COASTER LIFE

Learning from Thomas how to communicate authentically, right from the heart, has allowed a lot of my life challenges to feel like a blessing. There is a silver lining or as I like to call them GEM's (God Empowering Moments or God Empowering Me). Despite all that life put in front of me, the spiritual wake-up calls like the roadblocks, the hits across the head with the "cosmic" two-by-four, or the brick wall, whatever metaphor you like to use, there is something, someone that embraces it all. Some may call this God, some may call it Divine Presence, the universe. I am calling it a presence of divine faith that all is well with the world. It just is. It's an amazing sense of unconditional love, peace, and stillness.

We all encounter life challenges along our life journey. It's the way you choose to deal with them that is the important thing.

For years, actually decades, when I was faced with a challenge, I would take a deep breath in and just get up and on with it. Maybe you notice, I didn't write a deep breath out … I really don't feel I have properly breathed out much of my life. I was breathing shallowly just like I was experiencing life. Anyway, my emotions related to any of these life challenges or daily living were literally being stored in my body. I began to know all these emotions as my emotional backpack. Yes, I could feel the heaviness, the burden on my back and shoulders as well as other parts of my body. Finally, the backpack was so heavy, I needed to take action and deal with the emotions. Thank you to all the transformational tools I learned. These tools are part of me and my daily practice, serving me well to be thriving in this life. Please refer to the appendix at the back of the book.

There are still challenges. At times I think I can control them but who am I trying to kid? Fortunately, I am experiencing such calm, stillness and joy in the eye of the storm, that life delivers. This allows me to accept what is in that particular moment.

WOULD YOU HAVE HAD IT ANY OTHER WAY?

There have been many life-changing days, or probably moments, in my life. One of these particular moments was when a yoga teacher said to me, "Would you have had it any other way?" She was referring to everything to do with Thomas contracting meningitis and the challenges this one particular event brought forward in my life. My answer shocked me, yet it was the truth. What I said was, "I wouldn't wish pneumococcal meningitis on anyone, definitely not my son. However, given that he did contract meningitis, I am a far better person for it. I know this to be true as I would not be doing what I am doing now if that life-changing event had not happened." So, the short answer is "No."

For much of my life, I had no opinions about most things, but I had to have a very strong reaction to be provoked enough to say something. You might say if I felt there was an injustice, I would speak or act.

SHIT HAPPENS AND THEN ... OUTSIDE THE BOX

In this life of mine, my soul has chosen to experience a lot of life's challenges. I am not saying this to seek pity or sympathy from you, the reader. No, not at all. I am saying this as I now know, in each of the challenges I have received significant personal growth. I know that in darkness there is light; in sadness, joy, and in despair, hope.

Within each and every challenge, there is a gift.

Shit happens in life. Life has taken me in many different directions depending on my choices made in that moment called now. Life has guided me into a way I couldn't even have conceived. It's when I allow the possibilities of the unknown to come and then I am shocked at the ease at which it comes. This has been the journey for me.

When I put my conscious mind into action to think about the possibilities, I received a limited number of options. Yet, when I stepped into the stillness, the possibilities appeared to be infinite ... oddly enough, I hadn't thought of them.

I had forgotten that in this stillness, this universe, or however you define this infinite intelligence, presence is infinite. There is no way our mind could access all of this.

This presence is infinite. It keeps going. It's like love, divine love. Divine love is boundless … there is no boundary and it is unconditional.

There is a love that has boundaries. Boundaries of a body. I say "I love you" to my husband. I am meaning I love the body, mind, and soul that is him.

Divine love goes beyond this, beyond a sense of forever flowing. Like a fluffy white cloud as far as the eye and beyond. Or as the great Buzz Lightyear from *Toy Story* so aptly says "To infinity and beyond." We are connecting with the story of our soul. Our soul can feel like it is confined to our body, but it isn't. When I tapped into this sense, I could feel the possibilities were, indeed, infinite.

I love that fact and knowing there is a way life continues, just in a different form. The beauty, the sense of comfort, peace and contentment it gives me.

My growth has come from surviving the life challenges and experiences I have encountered and learning to thrive. I assist my son, Thomas, by listening deeply to his crying, his cries for help, his pain, his anger, and frustration. I watch his actions like a hawk or bird of prey circling his prey before the final descent. I see lack of action. I can see it all.

A mother's wisdom, a mother's connection to her young one, is wisdom birthed from the adventures and challenges of my life.

THE WORLD OF DISABILITY AND MENINGITIS

When I was 11 years old, I attended a boarding school called Columba College, about an hour from where my parents lived. Boarding school was to provide opportunities I couldn't access from living in a small country town with a population of no more than 2,000. One such opportunity was to be involved in a Red Cross group at school and volunteer in local charities. There were a wide range of charities in Dunedin, given its then population of more than 100,000.

Anyway, this particular day our Red Cross Group visited a centre for Intellectually Handicapped Children, called IHC. On this visit, a young girl probably a few years younger than I followed me around the playground. She just wanted to connect and show her love. You see, the girl who had Down Syndrome. I didn't know why I didn't want to connect. I felt uneasy, fearful, and couldn't wait to get out of there. The 11-year-old mind of mine was full of questions.

Why was this child following me?

Why is she close?

Why do I want to run away?

My body was feeling so much, and my mind had lots of questions, but I couldn't make sense of it. Fear was there and I had no idea. What I did subconsciously was store the fear away in my body until later in life when I would have the transformational tools and time to deal with my fear. I suspect I didn't speak to anyone about it, as I was ashamed by my reaction.

Roll the clock forward 21 years. In that moment, I collapsed on the hospital floor after hearing the doctors say the word "meningitis." My nine-and-a-half-month-old baby, Thomas, was in the Adventist Hospital Accident and Emergency surrounded by doctors and nurses. There was panic in the air. There were so many questions.

In that moment, I knew my son could die.

I knew my life was changed forever. Yet, I didn't really know what that meant.

It took time. It took decades for me to navigate this new world I found myself in. The world of disability with no prior experience except the one fearful experience with a young girl with Down Syndrome who wanted to connect and show her love.

Some two decades ago, nothing prepared me to be there by my helpless baby's side. I didn't want to admit that I felt helpless. I felt that God had deserted me. I questioned, "Why? I had been so good, done everything according to the way I thought it should be done. In the right natural order." Then I felt the doctors deserted Thomas and me as they could not fix him, put him back to the way he was before the meningitis.

I felt like everyone had deserted us. Therefore, the only solution was to take to fixing Thomas myself.

It seems crazy as I write this. It was true. I know parents out there reading this will be able to relate. I was desperate to do anything to fix my broken son, my broken Thomas.

The reality of mothering my young baby, boy, and ultimately adult scared me immensely.

SHOCK ... IT'S ALL ABOUT PURPOSE.

Immediately my mind questions this statement. "Is Thomas's illness really about my purpose? How can it be? How can his purpose be about enduring a trauma like this? How can it be about such sad times, times that weren't easy?"

Once I allow my mind its questions, the true pure answer arises.

"It's about unconditional love, and compassion for another. Assisting beyond assisting. Empowering and enabling."

Yes, there is shock within every cell of my body. There is a part of me wanting to resist writing about the shock of what happened to Thomas and shock at the reality I now faced.

Initially, I found hope with the angels and fairies.

I practiced the connection with my higher self. That deep wisdom. I loved being with the fairies and angels as everything there was rosy and light. I thought I was in my body, fully in my human body, but now I realise that the trauma, the shock was too great for me, so I spent a lot of time hanging out with the angels and fairies. This gave me so much lightness and peace, but I wasn't grounded in my body. I wasn't feeling those deep traumatic emotions. They were hidden deep within me.

I wanted everyone to join me in this rosy, light place. My intuition came into play. I started to trust it. Yet it was difficult bringing it into my everyday life.

Time was going to assist me, I hoped.

I was not grounded. I was not connected to the reality of life. Like I said, I didn't realise at that time I wasn't in my body. I had decided to disconnect from my body and pretend that all was well. All was perfect. I didn't need to feel my emotions if I chose to be out of my body. I didn't want to feel those so-called bad emotions such as terror, rage, shame, grief, anger, depression, desperation, hopelessness, and helplessness. I just didn't want to feel them. I wasn't allowing the good emotions either, such as passion, ecstasy, and joy. I now know there were so many emotions wanting to be felt, waiting for freedom. There was a queue of emotions waiting.

Eventually, when I was at my wit's end, my marriage was crumbling, a dear friend introduced me to the work of Brandon Bays. For more information on Brandon Bays refer to the appendix. Pandora's box was about to be opened. Nicky's box of emotional baggage and trauma was just waiting for the key to be released.

Pandora's box continues to this day. Today I am shocked by the shock. There is still shock in my body.

Shock can be ignited by the smallest of jolts. Recently, I was walking with David, busy in conversation, noticing a man and his three dogs in front of us.

A thought popped into my mind: *I noticed you yesterday, but you only had two dogs. I wonder where the third dog was yesterday.*" As my thought concluded, I tripped over my own feet. Fortunately, at the same time, my husband's quick reaction stopped me from landing flat on my face on the concrete path.

Sometimes, you need support even when you don't think you need support. I believe this is the time for mentors or having someone you trust who can mirror and guide you when things may not make sense. They can guide you back to yourself. They can remind you to return back to your centre, your aligned contained self.

That jolt reminded me to be back in the present, not pondering random questions with no relevance but to be truly present to walking, enjoying my husband's company, and the fresh air.

I was especially grateful as I was about to go on a writing retreat and having a broken arm/hand would have been less than ideal.

Now back to the shock of meningitis. This shock has been within me since 1998. It's not only the meningitis shock but shock from other childhood challenges. Just now as I am writing about it, giving it a voice, there is something freeing, something loosening up to allow space for something new. Now that's liberation. That's freedom in the making.

So, know that all is well. There is no need to be any particular way. All emotions are welcome. All emotions are energy life-force passing through the body. When I give my emotion a story, I get hung up on my emotion taking longer to move through my body than had I not given it a story. I had a lot of stored emotions, some very frightened, to reveal themselves.

My early years modeling/conditioning was to "just deal with it," "to get up and get on." It included even those childhood upsets that needed to be felt but weren't. Such experiences include when my pet lamb, Nibbles, should have won a pet prize at the local Agricultural & Pastoral Show and didn't. I didn't feel the sadness and deep injustice of that. You see what I am saying? The simplest childhood injustices needed to be felt and forgiven. If these childhood emotions are not felt and let go, they are stored within our body. For me, my emotions were collected in what I call, my "emotional backpack," gradually getting heavier and heavier with emotions I have stuffed away until I got a wake-up call. Examples of this:

When our pet rabbits escaped from their purposely built hutch. I didn't feel the loss of my pet rabbit.

When I started to attend boarding school, one of their rules was boarders could only see their parents three times a term. I didn't feel the sadness then. I held that sadness within.

These are some simple examples of when I didn't feel what I was feeling. My strategy was, just deal with it or just get on with it. I got up. I got on. This strategy supported me, until it didn't. It was when all the stored emotions became too much for me to carry and function in the world the way I wanted to function in the world. My emotional backpack was too heavy and overflowing.

Now I realise I had so many emotions and repressed memories stored within the cells in my being, which was not a healthy way to be. The weight of repressed and stored emotions became heavier and heavier as the years went on. I needed to unpack my emotional backpack.

I was like a simmering pot with the lid on. At any moment, the lid would lift briefly and out would spit resentment, anger, any repressed emotion at someone. It wasn't anything to do with them, but at the time, I made it about them. I made it their fault because they had done something to me. I was taking no responsibility for what I was doing. No responsibility for my part of the situation I found myself in.

Fortunately, with this deep lesson learned, it set me up for openness and a willingness to accept, respect, and love differences.

CELEBRATING DIFFERENCE

David and I celebrate our differences, laugh about these differences, and also celebrate the things we have in common. There is joy in this life. Communicating how we feel. We didn't have to be the same. We didn't have to be aligned in everything. There is a mutual respect, acceptance, and love for each other's uniqueness.

Me, being a woman on a spiritual path, helping others to find their stillness, their intuition, and see their own uniqueness and inherent gifts, along with their children's.

David loves flying and instructing others to be their best, the best they can. This brings him so much joy. This isn't in an arrogant way (maybe in the past it could have been but now was different), it's in a caring, compassionate way.

There is an opening for each of us to support the other in our dreams. Each of us supporting others to be their best selves. Currently, I am supporting David to realise his dream of flying again. This has meant relocating to the United States of America. This didn't happen overnight. There was much to consider. The children, their ages, leaving them, stable education for Greg as well as knowing David and my lives were moving on, being on the other side of 50, we wanted to fulfil our dreams, too. Thomas was already settled into a home with three other young men. I felt he was moving forward with his independent life, so I felt it was my turn. It was so difficult to even contemplate this, but I did. I made a decision and committed to myself, to Thomas, Alicia and Siân that I would travel back to New Zealand at least four times a year. It was a challenging and growth time for all of us. It meant I would have a foot in both countries. Sometimes I felt torn. Ultimately, it was what my heart and soul wanted to do. So I did. Going to the United States of America would give us the opportunity to be a couple and David to fulfil his dreams. I was there to support him and fulfill my dream of living in America. Other than that, it wasn't about me. Or so I thought.

My first year in America was a year of losing myself again. Trying some different things like competition tennis and painting. Only to realise some things were working for me while others were not. It was a wonderful year of adventure within and outside of America. A year I was very fortunate to have, as it reminded me what was important to me.

I loved playing tennis again. It is a sport I love. I so enjoy the connection with it, the love of hitting the ball so crisply and cleanly. The pure joy of it. Also hitting that sweet spot on the tennis racket while serving for the ball to land with perfect placement on the service line just by the T section. Such bliss and joy. I felt the connection with my Mum, as she played tennis and loved it. I could swear she was there with me.

Also, I connected with the fact she had felt she needed to give tennis up when she started a family. There was a palpable feeling of resentment around it and somehow, I was playing to play out that resentment for her. As soon as I allowed that resentment to pass through me, it was as if I released that stored resentment that was tucked away in my DNA. At the same time, I realised that although I loved tennis, I did not love the competition that came with it.

Also, with Thomas and my daughters, Alicia and Siân, living in New Zealand, I travelled back to New Zealand five times that year. This meant my availability for competitive tennis was spotty at the best, so I didn't get to play with the team much at all. In fact, it was only once. I believe I hold the 100% winning record at the club, winning the only match I played. Ultimately due to my family commitments, I decided not to put my name forward the following year. It was the right decision for me. In allowing that space, I reconnected with my true hopes and dreams, things that empowered and moved me forward with my dreams. That said, I hope I will play more socially in the future.

Initially, there was no love, acceptance, and respect from David's children. This took a lot of time and lots of tears and deep breaths, both in and out. Patience, compassion, and understanding. At times, I wondered if it was just too difficult to go further.

Give up, Nicky, said my internal voice. Yet my heart pushed on. It motivated me as did the support of David. He was solid. He was fully there.

All the kids challenged us both, starting from a few months after we met. Alicia, Thomas, Siân and Greg. All of them tested us individually and as a couple, in their own ways. I really don't need to go into the details. Enough to say, they were teenagers. They pushed every boundary they could think of. Fortunately, time passes, and time is a wonderful healer. They have all grown up. Three of them are more than 20 now. Just Greg, who wanted a book to be written about him, still challenges us. The teenage hormones, testing boundaries are being played out to the fullest. He knows he has only a short time until he is 18, when he can legally start making his own decisions and take responsibility for them. This is how it has been for Alicia, Thomas, and Siân. Being the eldest, Alicia has probably pushed the most for things. I can relate to this as I am the eldest of my siblings, too. Because of my failures and challenges, I believe my sisters got an easier ride. What crusaders the eldest children are … we pave the way for the younger siblings. Also, parents are practicing parenting on the eldest. I guess that is what David and I were doing with Alicia. Sorry, Alicia, for the mistakes I made. Dad and I were doing the best we could with the resources we had.

I am pleased to write that, now we have a lovely relationship. It has taken a lot of work on both sides. It was probably taking a good three years to work through the challenges. I am not saying all is rosy. I am saying we have arrived at a place where I feel there is mutual respect for each other. There is mutual acceptance for each other and a mutual love for the roles we are playing in each other's lives.

The wonderful relationship we have as a family is not to take away the grief and sadness that exists when you lose a parent at such an early age. I feel sad that Alicia, Siân and Greg lost their Mum. I didn't know Karen, may she rest in peace. I do know the sadness of losing a Mum. My mum passed away 10 years ago. I felt I lost her too early, too. I feel cheated of at least a decade with her. But it wasn't as early as Alicia, Siân, and Greg lost their mum. It is what it is and what life has dealt them as children. Sad but true.

I had always wanted more children, and even thought about adopting a child when I was separated from Thomas's dad, Bill, and single in Hong Kong. I did some initial investigating. I believe at the time, the adoption agencies told me that I needed to be divorced or married. I was in the process of divorce, so I decided not to start the adoption process. I felt rejection from the adoption agency. How could they not want someone like me? Fortunately, that subsided, and I knew my divorce was enough to cope with. This was so unlike me, as I seemed to thrive on the drama of life. Honestly, I thought there was an opportunity to have more children naturally. Indeed, I did become pregnant when I was divorced from Thomas's dad, Bill. I believe this pregnancy assisted me to find who I really wanted to be and who I didn't want to be. Unfortunately (at the time), I miscarried early in the pregnancy. There was grief in this. The loss of a dream for me. As time moved on and I surrendered into what was, I was at peace with the miscarriage.

I know if I had been totally wanting an adoption, I would have gone for it. Something was not ready or aligned, or indeed there were other options available to me. I would consider those options when I could know my life and direction had a lot more certainty.

I remember having a card reading with a healer. Thank you, Christine. You are an angel. She said there was another way to have more children, not of you but by marrying someone who already had children. This didn't feel like a viable option for Thomas and me as I felt I didn't have the capacity for energy, love, and resources as a whole to take on the responsibility of someone else's children. Yet I remained open to the possibility.

There was a part of me that wanted to give birth to another young bundle of joy. I played with this idea in my mind for years. Even at the wonderful age of 47, when I met David. We explored the potential of having a child together. We danced a dance with this for several months before finally making a decision not to and David took the brave step, as many men have before, to make it a permanent situation.

David and I are both blessed with four wonderful children between us. Our four children are giving and filling us with all the love, joy, and challenge we could manage.

Finally, after time, patience, compassion, and joy did come to our family unit. I vividly remember the day everything shifted. I felt like someone had waved a magic wand and joy and laughter was upon us. The whole family, including Alicia's and Siân's boyfriends, Thomas's two support workers, Richard and Karina, and the whole family had a joyous day at Rainbows End, a small theme park in Auckland, New Zealand. Sometimes we experienced rides together, other times the ones who loved thrill seeking experienced the more challenging rides, while the rest of us watched. Other times we watched Thomas, Richard and Karina on rides. Sometimes Thomas enjoyed the rides, even taking into consideration a heightened risk of seizures.

We were all there having fun as a family. This was the point when we as a family turned the corner. It was the point I started to see things differently with our family unit.

More acceptance, more respect, more unconditional love.

I haven't actually spoken to them about this. I know I will in the future. Maybe it will be through this book that I will do this. Maybe it will come up when we next holiday together. It's all part of the journey.

HEALING FOR THOMAS

I remember a time, when I was learning to be a "Journey Practitioner," Thomas was particularly unsettled. On this occasion I was lying down beside him as he slept. I connected with him through a technique I had learned and was practicing, The Journey. Through this process, I got clarity that Thomas actually didn't like the black and white mobile I had above his head in his cot when he was a baby.

I remember reading in books all those years prior, "What to expect when you are expecting," "What to expect in the first year," "Toddler years, etc.", that for young babies black and white mobiles were the most appropriate, slowly moving onto colour mobiles when they were older babies. This was probably specified in months, but I can't remember that exactly. I have allowed a lot of that knowledge to go but no doubt it will return when I enter that next phase of life of being a grandparent.

Now in this Journey process with Thomas, he was showing me a different way. It was going to be Thomas's way. His way or the highway. Through the Journey process, Thomas was able to let me know his feelings on the black-and-white mobile and be able to come to a place of forgiveness. Such a beautiful peace and calm came over Thomas and me.

I needed to accept that Thomas was expressing his desires and it was best to follow his lead. It took me years to understand

and accept this. I still challenge this knowing and rest assured, reader, it is Thomas's way or things aren't easy and I would be setting myself up for a lot of struggle and stress.

TRUST LIFE'S JOURNEY

Trust Life's Journey is my first published book. In it, I share an honest and raw account of the struggles and triumphs of being a mother of a young boy with disabilities. I share Thomas's and my story of how our worlds turned upside down, spun us around and spat us out on a road with no map, no plan, and totally disorientated into a world I didn't have a clue about. The world of disabilities. The world of lifelong challenges. I shared my vulnerabilities from my perspective in the hope it gave courage to others to share their vulnerabilities. I also invited my friends, family, therapists, and doctors to contribute their perspective of what had happened to Thomas and the effect it had on them and their loved ones. Some of them chose to contribute. You will be able to read their contributions in that book. The purpose of the book wasn't about getting sympathy or pity. It was about sharing my struggles and triumphs as a way to give others hope. You are not alone. To share the message that there is actually light at the end of the tunnel, even when it may not seem like there is. The light may be different from the light you expect, but nonetheless it is light.

Maybe Thomas and I are hope-deliverers to you, the reader.

IT WAS ME ON THE FRONT COVER. NOT THOMAS.

Only recently, I finally recognised I have always retreated. I have searched for a hidden room or a quiet space, to allow either further study or search for answers, whether it be for my school subjects or the deeper questions in life.

Even in 2014, when I was publishing my first book, *Trust Life's Journey*, I had about six possible designs for the front cover. I ended up choosing the cover about which I had the biggest emotional charge. It also happened to be the one most of my friends and trusted advisors preferred. That front cover is in the back of this book, for your reference. Have a look. The cover has a young boy in the glass box. I thought it was Thomas. I now know in truth, it was actually me. I had put myself into a glass box. This realisation resonated deeply with me and I have been able to shatter the box and now let go of the bounds it held.

I have realised that I don't need the books to hide behind. I don't need more information for my mind. I realise I have needed to quiet my mind to allow the stillness, to listen to my heart.

As I have quieted my mind, it's about clearing up my thoughts, clearing and letting go of what no longer serves me, to be a clear vessel for what is needed to come through for me. It's the truth of it.

Less is more.

COMMUNICATION HIS WAY

As you may know, Thomas was born a perfect, healthy young baby. He contracted pneumococcal meningitis when he was just nine-and-a-half months old. He nearly died because of the meningitis. This illness left Thomas with a number of lifelong challenges such as epilepsy, bilateral profound deafness, brain injury, global development delay (a label given when a child takes longer to meet developmental milestones than other children of a similar age), and left-sided hemiplegia (a condition caused from brain injury like meningitis, that results in a weakness and stiffness in the body).

One of my major concerns was, how was I going to communicate with my son? How was he going to communicate with me?

There was a long list of communication methods, of traditional therapies. They were tried and tested with very positive results for others. But not for Thomas. He would improve with each method for a while, then arrive at a plateau. There he would remain. Thomas wouldn't embrace any of these methods to move beyond the initial plateau. It felt as if he were pushing us to find some new innovative way for communication.

With the open-mindedness and thinking outside of the box, a dear friend, Tracy-Kim Gilchrist, a Speech Pathologist, found a way, Thomas's way. A way totally guided by Thomas and surrender. At this moment it is not a precise science. It is not a communication system for idle chit-chat. It is a communication system that speaks truth from the heart about what is going on for Thomas and for the people he has a photo of. I am in awe of his connectedness to his heart and the heart of the people he reacts with. We continue to develop and fine-tune his communication system.

This has been discussed in my second book *Communication His Way*. There is a description about it at the back of this book. In brief, *Communication His Way* describes how oracle and affirmation cards linked with photos have become a means of communication for Thomas.

The process is:

Thomas will take a printed photo of a client into his hands. He holds it as if he is connecting to the person in the photo. He will use blue tac – a reusable putty-like pressure adhesive to attach lightweight objects to walls, doors or other dry surfaces – to stick the photo to the wall, then will select a pack of Oracle/Affirmation cards to work with at that particular time. He will select one or sometimes a few cards to go with this photo. During the process, Thomas will sometimes place his hand on a client's photo and stills himself. It's as if he is sending healing energy to that particular person. I have witnessed his healing numerous times.

As I am writing, Thomas reminds me that this is the way he wants to communicate. He wants to help others know themselves better, deep within, to help them heal themselves. He has no interest in the mundane conversation of life. It's about authentic, real conversation from one heart and one soul to another heart and soul. This communication is such a huge blessing for me and my family and now to his clients. Yes, he has paying clients.

Here are some of the examples of the clear communication from Thomas.

1. Thomas drew a photo of himself with a puzzled look, placing beside it, an oracle card saying it is time to balance between exercise, good nutrition, and rest. I received this card reading so I think clearly Thomas needs his exercise, good food, and lots of sleep and rest. At this time Thomas was living in a house with three other young men with 24/7 care and support. The interesting thing is when I enquired into Thomas's routine at this time, it became apparent Thomas had had three takeaway meals in the past five days. I felt this was clear communication from Thomas I was to address this imbalance with his support workers. From my perspective, Thomas was saying he preferred to have different, perhaps healthier, food, more exercise, and rest. I understand that others may not see it this way. I am okay with that as long as they do not impede or disrespect Thomas's communication system.

2. In 2018, Thomas reconnected with a girl he met at his 17th birthday party back in 2014. A few years earlier, I asked his support workers to find this girl. I couldn't remember her name. Anyway, what happened was Thomas was matched with a girl the support worker thought I was talking about. Unfortunately, Thomas's support worker had matched him with the wrong girl. I searched again through my email for a photo, as I knew we had taken photos of his birthday celebrations. Eventually I found the photo of Thomas's 17th birthday party, the girl, and a date was arranged. Two days later while Thomas was with Richard and Karina (his private support workers), he drew the cards below. It just blew me away. Note it is a photo of Thomas below covered by one of the angel cards. There is a deeper story to this which will be revealed in one of my

upcoming books. It's a story of Thomas's persistence to reveal he had been matched with the wrong young lady. It will blow your mind.

3. Until I received the photo below, I had no knowledge that Thomas was being scratched by one of his flatmates so this reading enabled me to investigate further with Thomas's support workers. You will notice Thomas's angry face. He is obviously showing his anger about the situation. Fortunately, this angry photo doesn't come out that often. The second photo was the push for me to ask that a behaviour therapist be consulted as I knew he wasn't faultless in the scratching encounters. Thomas was seen by a behaviour therapist

supporting not only him but the support workers and family. Critical support for us all, especially Thomas, through some of his most turbulent times.

Also, in my second book, *Communication His Way* I discuss how Thomas's behaviour is a key indicator to his well-being and how he is feeling about life. At this time, I am not able to interpret each specific behaviour, but I am sure in time I will receive the understanding.

At this very moment, I smile to myself. I can feel that Thomas is patiently waiting. I have always said that Thomas can't wait. I guess in this case, I will have to say he is being very patient with me, waiting for me to be able to listen deeply and hear more clearly. There is more and more clarity as the days go by. I constantly feel in awe of my son.

Know that there are many times when I get very frustrated and angry with Thomas and myself that we haven't developed a 100% accurate communication system by now. As with everything in life, it's one step at a time.

And in Thomas's words, *"I am always here, Mum.*

"You can enjoy your life too, you know."

Such wise words from my son as I sometimes find the things I normally enjoy are a chore. It's time to take a break and breathe in and breathe out. Pause. Repeat.

And in the breathing in and breathing out and pausing there is stillness. Within this stillness, prayers do arise.

THE GP PRAYER

As I have mentioned, Thomas was diagnosed with pneumococcal meningitis in early July 1998. Fortunately, his General Practitioner (GP) took blood from him prior to giving him the medication he needed to survive in the Accident and Emergency Department (A & E) of Adventist Hospital, Hong Kong, so they knew when the doctors received the results what the bacteria was and how to treat it further. Because the best Paediatric ICU was in the teaching hospital, Thomas was transferred there. The irony of the situation was that we lived right next door to this teaching hospital. We had driven about 20 minutes by car to the Adventist Hospital as we had thought it would offer the best treatment for Thomas. We were wrong.

Thomas spent the next several weeks in Queen Mary Hospital. We monitored his input (bottled milk and soft solids, as I had just finished breast feeding), his output (yes, his urine and bowel movements) and anything in between. Even though he was not making progress, there was talk among the medical staff about discharging Thomas with a feeding tube. This was the way I was to manage his food intake. This totally scared me. I wasn't comfortable with this at all. I am not sure if it was what motivated us or Thomas's lack of progress or perhaps both, but we decided to search for doctors to give us a second opinion about Thomas's condition. After numerous referrals from friends and family in Hong Kong, we settled on Dr. David Chan to give us a second opinion on Thomas. Because of hospital policy, we had to take him on leave from Queen Mary Hospital and check him into another hospital which happened to be the original hospital, the Adventist hospital. We assumed it would be a day or two but again we were wrong. What the tests showed was that Thomas still had an infection in his meninges. The bacteria were still there.

I telephoned the teaching hospital to tell them what had happened and that we wouldn't be back, as Thomas needed to have a ventriculoperitoneal (VP) shunt operation. This is when the surgeon inserted a catheter into Thomas's brain with a valve placed under the skin on his head, attaching another longer catheter placed under his skin, behind his ear, down his neck, and into his abdomen. Initially it would be an external shunt until they knew how to treat the infection that was still active. Eventually an internal VP shunt was inserted. Again, Thomas was in ICU … hopeless and helpless, as was I. How much can you endure as a patient, as a parent?

Thomas appeared to make some progress after these operations, only to stagnate again after about a week.

Initially, Thomas was in a room by himself, which was great for privacy. I stayed most of the time with him. My sisters were staying at different times, supporting us at home, and at the hospital.

Another patient was admitted to the same room with a virus. It didn't make sense to me or the doctor, as there was a risk of further infection, but it was what the hospital did. Perhaps it was all about the business model and money.

Thomas wasn't making the progress the doctor and us thought he should be. Actually, Dr Chan was lost as to what to do. He said, "It is time to stop everything and get Thomas home."

Puzzled, I asked him why.

"Last night I had no idea what to do, so I prayed."

This totally warmed my heart. It was so liberating to hear him speak this way and he was willing to be open to what answer his prayer brought. What a blessing for his intuition to pray, to listen, to share, and to follow the answer.

In that moment, I knew the most appropriate action was to get Thomas out of the hospital and start his rehabilitation journey. And truthfully, it was the start of my rehabilitation journey too, a journey back to myself.

Dr. Chan granted us a "fit to fly" certificate so as soon as we could be organised, Thomas's dad, Thomas, and I were off to Auckland, New Zealand.

HIS SOUL'S CHOICE

There are so many beliefs we can embrace as a human being. I have explored many different beliefs over my lifetime. My life experiences have shaped and changed my beliefs, and I realise my beliefs may change in the future as life reveals itself. At this time, I believe I am a spiritual being having a human experience. My physical body is the home of my spiritual being in this lifetime.

I believe I have come into this life to be and experience many things.

Whether I (the spiritual being) planned my life to be exactly as it is, I am not sure. I certainly feel I am learning what I needed to learn at a great rate. The pace at which life is revealing itself to me appears to be fast, so it is even more important for me to remember to be still, to totally stop, open to what is, remembering to breathe in and breathe out.

Before I was able to feel into that place of stillness, I questioned everything. It wasn't always externally. Internally I questioned, why me? Why Thomas? Why my family?

Then the questions became: Why not?

After listening to Oprah interviewing Gary Zukav on her Oprah Show back in the late 1990's, my query changed. Oprah asked Gary Zukav, why God would allow a young baby to pass away. What had they done? It just doesn't seem fair. His answer was simple: "It was the baby's soul choice."

WOW. In that moment of hearing this, I totally got it. Something shifted in me. It wasn't what I had or had not done, it was Thomas's soul's choice to have this experience. So, it was mine as well. His soul's choice sank into my humanness. I gained so much peace from this statement.

Then not long after, one of Thomas's Hong Kong speech therapists said to me, "It's his soul's choice." I replied "Yes, I know." We both looked at each other and knew something extraordinary had just happened. We both recognised the truth. There was such acceptance in this. This therapist I have mentioned before, Tracy-Kim Gilchrist, is now a dear friend.

PART TWO

GIFTS WITHIN MY JOURNEY AND HOW TO

You got this. This is why you are here on earth. You are here to assist yourself, Thomas, and others who are in a similar situation. What I mean by this is parents who have a child/children with lifelong challenges. Even though everyone's situation is different, just like everyone is a unique expression of a human being, there are things we can do to assist ourselves, and our children so they can be living and thriving in life just the way they desire.

It is not about surviving life, having a half-life. It is about thriving and living a life you truly desire and all the dreams even beyond your imagination. This will connect with them. It will allow them to reconnect to their inner self and to their truest desires.

I know that may seem impossible to you at this moment, as many have suppressed or forgotten their desires or just thought it isn't possible to fulfill your purpose of being a parent, let alone what you truly want to do in your life.

DESPERATION TO INSPIRATION

"The world is a richer place when we are reaching our potential." – Nicola Irvine

How are you, the reader dealing with shock in your life?
How does it play out in your life?
Do you even know what I am saying?
Do you want more peace, clarity and freedom in your life?
Do you feel there is a deeper calling for your life?
Do you feel you are meeting your potential?
Do you feel you are guiding your children with respect, love, and acceptance?

My journey has been a different journey, a different parenting journey from many. This doesn't make it better or worse than anyone else. It is my experience of life, my experience of being in this life of mine. It is real. It is true. It is the truth of the way I view life in this moment. The preciousness of this moment. The pure joy of the moment of this way of being. I can't believe it.

Are you at one with yourself?

Are you getting, and giving what you want with life?

Do you have the desired joy and love in your life?

Do you have a sense of purpose that is yours and yours alone? Not someone else's, not your child's, not your husband's/partner's nor your parents?

A purpose that is truly yours.

It is time for you.

It's time for you to claim your life

There was a time when I wasn't living life for me.

I was living life as a caregiver.

I made no time for me.

I had not connected with my deepest desires and wants.

I had relationships that weren't healthy and honouring of who I desired to be.

I was in shock, paralysed by shock for decades.

I was exhausted physically, emotionally, mentally, socially, and financially. Totally spent in all ways.

I wasn't living my life.

I was living life as a caregiver, putting all my needs, wants, desires totally to the side.

I wasn't thinking about my spirituality.

When did I finally get it?

There wasn't one moment when I finally got it. It was a process of remembering who I really was and letting go of strategies, habits, and patterns that had kept me safe and secure. I faced my fears. As the fear loosen its grip, my life was about finding purpose and meaning for me and then I could have the resource to help my son.

There were a number of events that led me to where I am today. Life has led me to be here.

I must say I had wise friends who have guided me through this sometimes very rocky, twisted, hike of life. They assisted me to look at what I wanted in my life, to connect me with my desires, my intuition so I could move, take inspired steps toward all that I desired, creating clear boundaries. They have been my angels of support.

As I did this, I noticed I was more energised and available for my son to assist him with what he desired. This was to be of service by offering his services as a photo energy reader to others; a way for him to generate an income for himself from others. Thomas is able to read someone's energy from their photo. Then he connects with their heart. He will select an oracle or affirmation card/cards for them to reflect on. With support, Thomas will be able to achieve what he desires, his hopes and dreams can be fulfilled.

By my creating space for myself, space has opened for Thomas. It was perfect. It was a win-win situation for him and for me.

I can now see my boy graduating, graduating into a business owner.

The fortunate thing is, I arrived here where I am today, in a place of opportunity not only for me but for my son, Thomas. Yes, we are having our cake and eating it, too.

I can be fulfilled and purposeful, assisting others by sharing my stories via speeches, books, videos, and one-to-one mentoring. Thomas, too, can have independence physically and soon financially. He is a taxpayer. Yes, he needs support from the government for his care, but he has a small business and is starting to support his needs. He is fulfilling some of his needs and desires. He is meeting his potential.

You can do this, too.

Allow this day to count for making differences you want to see in the world.

The world is a poorer place without our loved ones finding their potential and their purpose.

YOU, TOO, CAN DO IT

Just as Thomas said to me in those early hours of my book-writing retreat.

"You, too, can do it."

You have your hopes and dreams. Your hopes and dreams in their truest of forms. They are not the hopes and dreams of your ego or personality but the hopes and dreams deep in your soul. That deeper calling. The soul desire that will keep you full to overflowing.

By connecting with the "internal me" I mean my soul. I opened to the possibilities not just for myself but also my loved ones.

Sometimes we don't want to acknowledge what is in the deepest, darkest corners. We assume it is bad. We have a judgment about our emotion, our memory, or our perspective. In that deepest, darkest corner is the essence of what is needed or required for you to unlock the potential not only in yourself but in others.

By being the best you, by being fully you, you give others permission to do and be the same.

You are not to be focused on others first.

I was focused on Thomas, not myself.

I felt self-care wasn't even an option for me. That's why I burnt out.

I wanted Thomas to fit into my hopes and dreams of what I wanted for him.

I wanted Thomas to fulfill my own personal dreams. (How often do you hear that parents push their children to do or be what they themselves wanted to do or be? Far too often, I would say.)

I wanted Thomas to be who I wanted to be or do.

In some way I thought I could control the shaping and forming of his life.

My mind rationalised this by thinking thoughts like these:

Because I had been good, only good things will happen to me.

Because I had done everything in the way deemed normal order… such as dated … engaged … married … had a child, only good things will happen to me.

Just because I was who I was, I thought it all should be exactly how I expected it to be.

There was no understanding, appreciation and acknowledgement that I wasn't in control of me and my family's and my son's destiny. In some way because of all of these reasons, I just assumed that life would go according to Nicky's mind/ego or as one of my spiritual teachers says, according to "the Nicola."

The connection I have with Thomas has been life-changing for me. The most transformational moment in my life is when I thought my son was going to die. Yes, his whole meningitis illness and his resulting lifelong challenges have taken my life into a direction I never, ever, thought was possible. Far beyond my wildest dreams.

How can you go from a place, where you are at the top of a mountain with all that you desire: a husband, a beautiful son, and all the material items? Yet my life was starting to crumble. My mountain was starting to crumble. Know that … I have experienced it. Now I am here to share that you can not only survive but thrive. You can. It can be done. I am here to deliver that hope. You just need to have the faith and trust life will unfold in the best possible way for you and your loved ones.

I also sensed life wasn't meant to be this way and there was something else.

I found a way, a way over a few decades to a place where I am more joyous than I have ever been, and I know that the best is yet to come. Not pushing an outcome, but from a knowingness that as things are being peeled away like layers of an onion and falling away like rocks that fall away as you climb a mountain to where forgiveness comes, guilt, regret, and jealousy dissipates, and there is such love, joy, acceptance and compassion.

The fullest of life appears from feeling the fullest of emotions.

EMOTIONS

What are emotions? They are energy in motion. It's not about attaching a story, blaming someone or something else, or suppressing the emotion. It's about feeling your emotion in your body.

Sometimes memories can come to the surface from your consciousness or in your mind. There are ways to address the memories but if you can stay with the raw emotion, and allow it, it will pass.

As Rumi says, **"This, too, will pass."**

I will give you an example from my life. I felt anger but I called it frustration. I believe I did this because society has so many negative associations with anger. I now know that anger can be used as fuel for your passion and create huge motivation to make change. From my experiences, I have realised that below frustration was some emotion that was even deeper, such as anger and rage. I believe my confusion around emotions was that I really didn't have a sense of what I was feeling as a child. I didn't know what my emotions were. I was taught or I observed my role models and community, to get up and get on. So, as a child, I got up. I got on.

Emotions come from within. But other people, circumstances, and events can trigger your emotions. Note that if you are triggered, the emotions are still within you. Just because Thomas behaved badly and I was angry, Thomas didn't cause me to be angry. It is my anger and my anger alone. It was up to me to address all the stored and suppressed anger and other emotions I had suppressed throughout my life.

I had to find a way to get these emotions out of me. Not that I was consciously thinking that. I just knew I was not as happy as I could be, and I needed to do something about it. In my years of living, there have been many situations and events, very traumatic events, that I was unable to deal with at the time. I suppressed my emotions as I knew I had to get up and get on.

So, the search begun.

It wasn't until Thomas's illness and prognosis had overtaken me, did I realise that Thomas had started to trigger and stir up every kind of emotion within me.

He was the one person in my life who stirred up the good, the bad, and the ugly. I admitted to myself that he triggered the depths of darkness to the oneness that feels that you are at one together with absolutely no separation.

Do you have a person in your life who triggers or stirs up emotions within you? From the depths of despair and hatred to an uncontrollable rage? Are you able to admit this to yourself?

Do you have a person who you love dearly and yet you know you can no longer live with them full time?

Is this the same person?

If the answers are yes, this person is probably your Thomas.

My Thomas has been, and will no doubt continue to be, my greatest teacher.

My Thomas has been, and will no doubt continue to be, my greatest inspiration in life.

My Thomas has helped me find the "me" I had forgotten, the "me" hidden between the suppressed emotions and trauma. He has helped me navigate my way back to my soul.

Your Thomas may be your loved one, your child, your mother, father, sister or brother, or any other relationship. Really anyone who evokes the deepest emotions within you.

I had to get honest with myself.

That is the first step.

By being honest with yourself about what you truly feel, you create awareness. And as Eckhart Tolle says, **"Awareness is the greatest agent for change."**

I knew Thomas was triggering me. I knew I had to listen deeply to what he wanted to say.

He couldn't say it through his words (well in words that could be heard through my ears), so I had to find another way.

I had to observe his behaviour.

I had to listen to what sounds he was trying to make, even though it just felt like he was screaming at the top of his lungs to try and get my attention. For me to give him my undivided attention and not listen with my ears … but listen with all of me … I had to listen with my heart and my soul. I had to listen to my own thoughts and feelings as well.

I had to be aware of his seizures, when they were, where were they, what was triggering them? I thought his seizures were the brain firing a response from brain injury and trauma but what I have realised for Thomas is when he is not coping well emotionally with what is happening in his world … whether the support worker isn't supporting him the way he would like … he doesn't like someone's energy … he doesn't want to do something … or just generally not happy, he will have seizures. This is one of the ways he releases built-up energy.

I have learned this over his life. Knowing this has taken time, patience, and a willingness to witness and observe what is happening. Reaching for beyond what is obvious....

So how have I done this?

PROJECTION

At the time of writing this, I am in my study on a virtual writing retreat. My husband, David, and son, Greg, are in the living room. They know I am on a retreat. I know I have asked them to respect this and be as quiet as possible. But yet, I can hear them. Their deep voices. It is starting to irritate me; I even begin to feel anger arise. This is a part of me that doesn't want to get angry, yet I am.

I want to go out into the living room, yell at them to be quiet and respect my demand to be quiet.

Yet, I am held back to feel my anger. I feel it move through my body. I am not attaching any story to the anger, although I could. I see this as an invitation for me to feel my anger and fall deeper into my writing retreat.

The anger passes and I continue with my writing. I did ask David about it later when I wasn't angry. He told me they had been making an effort. Just imagine if I had gone out and yelled at them when in fact, they were making an effort.

A reminder that it's my anger, not theirs, so it was mine to deal with.

May I ask you some questions ....

Do you blame others for how you feel?

Do you project your emotions out at others?

If you do, do you remember to say sorry?

Then do you remember to forgive yourself and let go?

I ask myself these questions.

If the answer to the first two questions is yes, you have work to do on realising that your emotions are *your* emotions. Yes, people can trigger an emotional response in you, but it's your choice how you react and respond.

Ultimately, we want to be in a place where we are aware of what is triggering us. Take responsibility for your emotions and neither project, blame, or suppress. This is a skill that takes time and patience with yourself.

Even as I write this, I started to go into the story of how my husband and son were affecting my virtual retreat. I know I could have gone outside and blown my gasket. In the end what would that have achieved?

Nothing.

It would have resulted in everyone being angry. Both David and Greg thought they were being thoughtful and respectful, honouring my earlier request to be quiet.

I was so thankful I didn't act out of impulse and anger. Instead, I allowed my emotion. This was a true example of what I was writing about. What has happened for me is that I was able to continue my writing, falling deeper in the process of the retreat, and they stopped being so loud … according to my ears, of course.

As a result, I have allowed my anger to move through me. Anger was allowed, not suppressed … it didn't need to be stuffed away in my body for another day. My anger came and my anger went.

Just like every other emotion is meant to do ... energy in motion.

It has taken me years to create awareness and stop my automatic response pattern. One day I may become a master at it. In saying that, I know we are humans and humans make mistakes. I hope I am making those mistakes less and less.

SUPPRESSION

The other option is to suppress your emotions and just carry on with what you are doing.

I know this reaction well, as I have done this for decades. I am here to tell you, eventually life catches up with you. Those stored, suppressed emotions need an outlet.

For me, my body started to be impacted.

- I was burnt out.
- I didn't have the energy I used to have and wanted to have.
- I started to cover up things … telling those little white lies you tell to not only yourself but also to friends and family.
- I started to increase my intake of alcohol.
- I started to go out and party.

Finally, I decided to go to my doctor. I found out my blood pressure was high. I knew I didn't want to depend on medication, so I had a choice to make.

I decided to look into other therapies. They have all helped my well-being. Now I can say I have blood pressure well within the normal parameters and no medication has passed my lips. That's not to say I was so close to taking medication.

It has taken much financial resource, it has taken time, patience, and determination to have the support in a less intrusive way.

It has taken me years to actually feel my suppressed emotions. There are still times I don't, and I am able to catch myself … yes, a reminder to self that I am human.

When should you start?

I had to start at the beginning. I couldn't identify a lot of feelings I was having. I knew in my mind what was good, bad, sad, and happy but what was anxiety, hopelessness and helplessness, ecstasy, despair and rage? I really didn't have much emotional intelligence. I had packed them away, suppressed them in my body.

I was fortunate enough to find a safe group of friends, a community who could support me in allowing these emotions to be felt. Initially, it was totally foreign to me. But the sense of relief, peace, and stillness and expansiveness, the all-encompassing feelings I felt when I had previously felt the "so called negative feelings" such as anger, rage, hopelessness, grief, was so liberating.

I started to have energy again.

I started to feel vibrant again.

I started to make better choices for my life and for my son Thomas's life.

THE PREPARATION - THE TOOLS OF MY LIFE

Over the decades of my life, I have experienced so much of life and what life offers. All experiences have enriched my life. There are often moments where I really cannot describe the impact those moments had on my whole being other than they were life-changing. I no longer see or speak of experiences being good or bad. They are just experiences, with some learning, a depth of understanding.

The transformational tools I have used have been found through searching for my purpose and finding out what I am really meant to be doing or "being," as it is in my case. Some may call it your soul's purpose. In the simplest form my soul's purpose is to BE. To be "me" in each and every moment.

As I mentioned, along my journey I have been blessed to meet a lot of teachers, healers, mentors, wise friends, and family offering wise counsel. These were transformational tools as well as new perspectives and healings. Through each and every one of them, I have learned much about myself, the world, and the universe in which we live.

The most inspirational teacher by far has been my son, Thomas. He is a master of the highest order, the highest calibre. Teachings of Master Thomas have pushed me to the depths of despair, hopelessness, and helplessness to the ecstatic joy of the simplest of moments/gestures like a moment where two hearts and souls breathe as one. There are those moments I connect into his eyes and I feel his divine love and wisdom. Or those moments when I receive a two-arms hug or that gentle peck on the cheek, as if an angel had brushed his wings along my receptive face.

As a result of my searching for my purpose and to make sense of what had transpired in my own life, I discovered transformational tools such as *The Journey* by Brandon Bays, *The Reconnection* by Eric Pearl, Art of Feminine Presence programme by Rachael Jayne Groover, Heart IQ programme by Christian Pankhurst, Donny Epstein's work and individual mentors. There is an appendix at the back of this book with details of each of these.

I opened myself to the techniques, tools, the enquiry within me, and found a peace, a stillness within that is difficult to describe. I know the stillness is there even among the trials and tribulations of daily human life.

There has also been much exploration into many different therapies and practices, which are now a part of me and daily beingness.

At this time, I enjoy my meditation and prayer; yoga, whether it be in a class with others or in the privacy of my own home; journaling about events that have invoked an intense emotional response or not; walking, preferably in nature, on a beach or near water; sitting in reflection and quiet contemplation in a garden or near water.

My wellness routine includes visits to an osteopath/networkcare chiropractor, a naturopath, an acupuncturist, a massage therapist, a mentor, and nourishing food. Also allowing time for the naughtiness of different foods such as ice-cream, chocolate, and potato chips as well as a glass or two of wine/bubbly or favourite cocktail.

The first self-inquiry transformational processes I encountered was *The Journey* - a series of processes pioneered by Brandon Bays. These processes are globally recognised healing and transformational methodology, opening my world. They revealed how I had been showing up in life and what life conditioning, wounds, and experiences had sent me on the particular direction my life has taken. It showed me that I wasn't being fulfilled in the way I wanted to be fulfilled. I needed to stop and have a good look at myself and the way I was living my life. I needed to be gentle with myself and start making changes so that new, refreshing, more joyous ways could be revealed. I could start to choose to show up in life in a different way.

Over time, my life changed, as did my relationship with fear, rage, and anger along with many more emotions I didn't even know existed. As I learned what I was feeling, acknowledged the emotions, and allowed them their voice, my anger, rage, and fear started to reduce, seemingly allowing room for joy, passion, and stillness and every other emotion. In saying this, I was actually learning what my feelings and emotions were. I had kept them so tightly held I really didn't know how each one felt. The emotion was either good or bad. That was in the days of black or white; you either knew or didn't know; the financial statements and accounts either balanced or didn't balance. It seemed to be simple, yet I was missing out on so much colour and vibrancy in my life and what life could offer.

I am not perfect by any stretch of the imagination. Anger, rage, fear, and those other emotions still arise but they tend to pass through quickly. My mind has always been an active mind. Fortunately, my mind is starting to know stillness, peace, and quiet. The need to know, the need to understand, is waning. Thank goodness, as there is so much to think about, too much to consider, to understand, to explain. It is so fabulous when you can allow the thoughts to come and go. It is a process, a process I will no doubt be mastering for the rest of my life. It is not a chore. It is a way of being, so I am allowing the best "me" to be present at this time.

There is a caveat. I am a spiritual being having a very full human experience, so my humanness does count. The humanness, the ego, does come in to play at times. More often than I would like. And the judger (that part of me that judges not only myself but others) likes to remind me that she is a part of me. I now know that is okay. I accept what is there in that particular moment.

I am so grateful for Brandon Bays and her teachings, *The Journey*. The platform, the community that resonated with me, supported me through a very terrifying phase of my life.

The Art of Feminine Presence programme has allowed me to heal a very old, deep, childhood wound and now so much more. It has allowed me to operate from a new centre, a new power point which has catapulted me into a place of focus, flow, and direction. My sense of purpose has crystallised so much that I can no longer write or speak casually. I need to do it vocationally and treat my purpose that way. Although I have been following Rachael Jayne Groover from Art of Feminine Presence for many years, I recently joined online courses and began attending live events. I feel being in the United States has allowed me the time and space to explore these practices more deeply. The power of the experiences has been divinely timed, as it could only be.

I started an Art of Feminine Presence course, based on principles written in Rachael Jayne Groover's book, *Powerful and Feminine – How to Increase your Magnetic Presence and Attract the Attention you want*. It was a course that was totally revealing to me how I had blocked my power centre. What I mean by centre is an area in my body where my body has particular energies and cellular memories. Because of a childhood trauma of mine, I had blocked and suppressed emotions in my lower abdomen. It was around my creativity, my sexuality and my power. Even though I had done other transformative work, I had not cleared this block. That isn't to say it couldn't have been cleared. My divine timing for this clearing was in 2018 using Art of Feminine Presence tools. My daily practice from early 2018 has allowed me to be able to reconnect with this area to know a power that has eluded me until that moment.

It was an online course that assisted me to break into my power centre the first time since the sexual abuse when I was about nine years old. I had shut down this power centre to keep myself safe. The course taught me a way to allow myself the time, energy, and then breathe into three major areas in my body. I could access my head, my heart, but my power centre wasn't available to me, until that moment. I struggled with the process initially. It took me weeks. Others in the course were having lots of breakthroughs but not me until David and I were on a road trip exploring south Florida in late January, 2018. I just loved the south, the air boat ride, and driving the Keys, until I felt unwell deep within my power centre. It was a deep menstruation pain, but even more intense. I wanted to drug it away, but I decided to surrender to the pain. I lay there in bed in total surrender, feeling the pain. I struggled at times. I kept with my exercise, breathing into my head, heart, and into the area as low as I could go, gradually edging closer to my power centre, millimetre at a time. I was in this cycle for a few days.

Then at last, I eventually arrived at my power centre. What a shift this created for me. The connection to this area in my body brought a new sense of self, of connection to everything being possible and would be possible. It was an opening I had never expected or anticipated. Words really don't explain how it felt to me … beyond words, in truth.

I loved this new sense of self. It was that I could stand up straighter, taller, feel connected to my purpose, my sense of being, and could feel very grounded in my energy and in my body.

I love this feeling.

It wasn't a need to look, search, seek, or anything else. Everything was here and available from this new sense of self and space. I celebrated in this. I was in awe of this.

These practices are still with me. They are part of my daily practice, almost integrated into who I am now. Life is good. Life is fulfilling all of this for me to be all that I am. I am full of joy for this.

Another person I have been following for many years was Christian Pankhurst, the founder of Heart IQ. It wasn't until I experienced a couple of Heart IQ workshops that I encountered a deeper understanding around beliefs that I thought were unacceptable or inappropriate. These experiences allowed me to operate more from a place of heart and compassion. I also got to witness and feel how the amplified field of everyone coming together as a heart-centred space, can allow healing not only of the person at the centre of the experience but everyone within the workshop. I know I have sensed the amplified field at other courses, but the field seemed to be more palpable when everyone sits in a circle.

But why have I needed to do these courses, invest a lot of time, money, and effort? My soul, my heart and my being have drawn me toward them for a reason, I am sure. But what reason? They have provided me a way back to me … the "me" that was hidden by life's challenges, dramas, conditioning, and the way I perceived these events.

MY PRACTICES

My regular practices are meditation, yoga, walking, and journaling. I schedule time in my day for them. I don't know what the meditation will reveal, what I will receive. Sometimes messages. Sometimes actions, sometimes clarity, sometimes a great sense of peace. There is no right way. Know you can't stuff it up. You totally can't stuff it up.

There will be times that things flow. There will be times when there is a constant train of thought. Just allow them to come and to go, to come and to go. It's about allowing them their moment and allowing them to go. This really honours them.

The walking for me is about energizing my body. Getting my blood and body moving. Also allowing myself to be open to what I see visually. Sometimes I see what is around me, other times I am lost in the moment, and it is like I am in a walking meditation, seeing myself in everything. Everything has a pulse. Everything is breathing, allowing, and moving with the flow of breath.

Yoga is about flexibility and strength and moving in those parts that I don't want to move. They get into those parts that I don't want to get into. The hidden gems, stuck within my hips, my thighs, and my stomach.

These are areas where I hold.

What are your areas?

Where do you hide your deepest darkness and lightest emotions?

That light within you is so very bright so wanting to light up the world. Also wanting to be directed into the purposeful place, a place of serving you and the world. I often feel emotions in my neck and shoulders. I feel the clicking as I move my neck and shoulders around. I move it and it frees up. It's good for just allowing the energy within my being to flow.

More recently I have realised my body needs more strength as I implement my plan of making more of an impact of the world. So I have incorporated strength training. Fortunately, the trainer offers the training over Zoom, as she lives on the west coast of America. I now include this session in my weekly routine with the intention of another session on my own once a week. Oh no, did I just say more push-ups, more abdominals, and more squats?

Journaling during the day allows the words to be written. Words wanting to be expressed and heard for others . . . or maybe it's just for me. It's about allowing the words an outlet. Just allowing writing, journaling to flow.

This is probably the practice I don't do as much as I could. It's the practice I am still perfecting. Actually, I am still perfecting the others, too. That's why they are in my daily practice.

These are my four major daily practices. How did I know what I needed? It's about trying different practices to feel their impact. All you have to do is be aware of how you feel.

IT STARTS WITH AWARENESS

There are many people in my life. I am surrounded by my family and friends, neighbours, communities and the wider community on earth and beyond. Each person in my community is able to affect me by their presence, their mood, their behaviour, their way of being, their words, and all that they are.

In a way they are like my angels on earth. They are here to interact, relate, and connect just as I am. If you can agree with this, then each and every interaction is an opportunity to learn about how others relate, interact at a deeper level and to understand yourself at a personal and soul level.

As I have mentioned I believe we are spiritual beings having a human experience. So, our humanness does play a role in our perceived experience.

When you may have a judgment or be triggered by others' behaviour, it gives you an opportunity to see beyond their behaviour and know there is an angel within them. Just as there is an angel within you.

This reminds me of Neale Donald Walsch's children's book, *The Little Soul and the Sun.* It is a beautiful story about just that.

Thomas has been my biggest angel. His challenges, his life, and his behaviours have triggered me enormously over the past two decades. They have allowed me to access all types of emotions, from the depths of rage, desperation, and hopelessness to divine love, joy, and ecstasy.

You see, I had suppressed my emotions. I held on tight to them. No reason other than I didn't know how to let them go after suppressing them for so long.

With support of transformational tools and techniques, I was able to identify that I was being triggered. It was my emotion. It wasn't theirs, so it was up to me to address my emotions. I had a choice to make.

Do I want to continue being triggered by this person, this circumstance, or event?

My answer: "No."

I could continue to:

- Project out at others, blaming them for what was happening within me.
- Suppress my emotions more and therefore add to my emotional backpack, which was getting heavier and heavier to carry.

Or make a change to actually feel my emotions.

I chose to make a change.

OWNING IT...TAKING RESPONSIBILITY

It was only when I started taking responsibility for my own part in life's challenges and trauma, for my choices, that I could see life's wonderful tapestry more clearly.

When I felt my marriage was crumbling, I knew I had to get real with myself. I was unhappy. I knew I had to start taking responsibility, taking actions, and finding my way back to me, the universal me, the me that is who I am. The inner wisdom, the intuition, the all-knowingness within.

I knew I had strong intuition. I knew I have made strong feelings, strong messages, in the past, but I didn't trust myself enough to listen to them. Why would I? I trusted my mind, figuring things out. I thought using my mind was the way to do life. I thought I needed my mind to plan, to figure it all out.

When I started to connect with my head, my heart, and my intuition, I began to get clarity on the way I saw things in the universe. I became less judgmental, less prescriptive. I came to experience less drama in my life.

Yes, shit happened, and shit still happens. What was different, though, was my reaction. Because a lot of my repressed emotions along with their cellular memories had been cleared, my reactions were not triggering very old, deep wounds. Don't get me wrong, I still have strong, deep emotions. I feel them in the realness of the moment I am in. There wasn't blaming or judging. It was time for being in the moment called now.

I love my life. I have had many experiences that others have not been blessed to experience. It is what it is. It is only after years of reflection and daily practices that I can truly feel and know this.

FEEL IT AND SPEAK IT

I now know how I feel. No one can argue with my feelings. I guess that for much of my life, I wanted to know the facts and figures, so my mind could be satisfied, and I could convince others. Then I started to realise I had feelings and emotions. Emotions that had been stored away in my emotional backpack or locked away deep in my cellular memory from incidents, experiences, and wounds from past years. These cellular memories held a key to unlocking all the past hurts, judgments, and generally how I had been showing up in life.

I could see that when others in authority or others who I thought had superior knowledge expressed opinions, I would discard my own thoughts and feelings and follow theirs. This was the case in respect to doctors. This is not me blaming doctors as I do have very good friends who are doctors. It's about how I related to them in the past, giving them God-like status.

I vividly remember being invited to a friend's charity cocktail function. There were many doctors there. I was in a deep conversation with a doctor about vaccinations. He just assumed that because Thomas had contacted pneumococcal meningitis, I wish I had vaccinated him. To his astonishment I said, "No." He was totally flabbergasted. "How could you not want to vaccinate your son?" he asked. He spent the next 20 minutes trying to convince me I should have wanted to vaccinate Thomas. In the end, to bring the discussion to a complete stop, I said, "I respect your professional opinion." I put my right hand over the centre of my chest, and added, "In my heart, it wouldn't be the right choice for Thomas." He wasn't able to add anything further to the conversation, so we parted company. I felt I honoured myself and Thomas, speaking what was my truth. There was something very liberating about that.

THE JOURNEY

The Journey process consists of many transformational tools that allows you to empty out all the stored, repressed stories and emotions, finishing at a place where you can let go, so you can forgive. Some processes are mentioned in *The Journey* which can be completed with a friend. There are also more advanced processes used by an accredited journey practitioner. Amazing to be in that place, a place where I was able to forgive that person, those people, God, from the bottom of my heart, deep down within my being and at a molecular level. At last, my cells could start healing from all the stored resentment, anger, rage, and every other repressed emotion I had held from my life experience.

The campfire process is one of the processes I learned as part of The Journey. What I did was I visualised a campfire in my mind's eye. I then brought to mind the person who may have triggered an emotional reaction within me. I spoke as if that person were in front of me and then I allowed that person to speak from that deep place inside them, speaking of what was happening for them and then allow the conversation to continue until there is a deep understanding and compassion for the other person and for myself. There are many other techniques and processes to assist in this "campfire," to help you to get to a place where you feel you can forgive not only the person who triggered you but yourself as well.

The freedom from The Journey processes was huge for me. I now realise I didn't need to physically say what was said to my old principal. I do believe that I could have done a journey process to let go and hear her side of the story, so I felt 100% complete with experience, 100% forgiveness. Through a process I was able to get to a place of understanding and compassion for who the principal was, who she was trying to be, and for her upbringing. My heart was opened to possibilities and not resentment. What a relief to let that go.

ME TIME, DREAMING AND FORGIVENESS

As I unpacked my emotional backpack, there were patterns of behaviour, strategies for coping and to be safe, ways of doing, controlling, manipulating, and calculating being revealed to me. It was difficult to take at times. I was in a process of accepting these not-so-pleasant parts of me. Many people call these parts Shadows. Shadows can be light and dark. If there are parts of you that aren't fully integrated within you, they are in the Shadows.

Each of the strategies, conditioning, and patterns were like threads of a tapestry or pearls on a necklace. As I addressed the strategies and challenged my beliefs, each thread or pearl had less of a hold on me. I started to sense life differently, in visual, auditory, and kinesthetic ways. Everything was becoming bright and clearer as to how I could be in life.

Now I could get the sense of what my true purpose was. I could indeed see how I had co-created a lot of the drama in my life by the way I chose to react to certain life events.

This isn't about being hard on myself, although I must admit the self-critic and self-judge had always played a big role in my life.

As my mind quietens, takes a well-earned holiday, my self-critical judge can take a well-earned break, too. And when

I find the self-critical judge rising, I can actually smile and welcome it. In welcoming it, it comes and after time, it goes. As I haven't resisted, it hasn't persisted. In the past I have not been so welcoming to the parts of me that I deem unacceptable or just not nice, resulting in the self-critic taking over and throwing me completely off what I was meant to be doing.

The threads, or pearls, are seen for what they are. As a thread broke, I could see how that particular thread represented a theme in my life tapestry, allowing freedom from that particular drama. I was discovering the GEMs in my life's journey.

DISCOVERING THE GOD EMPOWERING MOMENT (GEM)

I remember one day when Thomas was in hospital. He was so very sick. This was another time I wondered if Thomas really wanted to be in this life. A friend assisted me by sending some distance healing to Thomas as he lay on his hospital bed in complete stillness. The healing was one of protection. Protection from other illness and diseases and protection from energies that were not beneficial to him, with his body being compromised and not in a state of wellness.

While I was there with Thomas, I met a wonderful woman whose young son was terribly unwell, too. He had been in hospital for months and had hopes of leaving the hospital soon. We connected, and experienced an immediate rapport so much that we became friends. Also, we did end up collaborating at a charity – White Rose Family Foundation - together. By working together along with the other White Rose Family Foundation co-founders we were able to make a difference for some young children with challenges, as well as their families. If Thomas hadn't been in hospital at that time, and I hadn't been there with Thomas at that time, we wouldn't have met and been able to make that difference.

This is a clear example of how a seemingly horrible, life-challenging and threatening situation can create opportunities and potential. You have to be willing to see beyond the situation you are in.

Many of us would call it the silver lining. I like to call it a GEM (God Empowering Moment or God Empowering Me). It is about being in the moment, without control, without judgment or expectation that allows you to be receptive to all the wonderful opportunities to arise.

The charity work involved families and children who had a lot less financially than most in Hong Kong. The school was able to give us some facilities to help host some classes, after-school activities for the children who had challenges physically, mentally, emotionally, and socially but they were in tune and off the scale, spiritually.

I have always been a positive person but to see the silver lining and GEM with Thomas's illness and all his hospital visits, I needed like-spirited people around me.

FIND YOUR TRIBES

Your experience is your experience. I know I have wanted validation from my partners, my husbands, my family, and friends – yet it is my experience. No one can really experience my perspectives as they haven't been in my shoes, walked my life-hike. I know some people are able to empathise with or understand me, as their life experiences have been similar or they have a deep connection with me. And I am open to the fact that their perspectives are totally valid for them, based on their life experiences.

Late in 2018, I had a healing session with a therapist. The key takeaways from this session were that I needed to have alone time to refuel myself, so I had time to do exactly what I wanted to do. To find my tribe and remember to dance in the rain. I allowed more alone time but where was my tribe? Where could I dance?

My tribes were scattered all over the world. Thank goodness for international travel and the more carbon-friendly option, the internet and apps such as "WhatsApp" and "Zoom."

The different tribes support different aspects of my soul's purpose.

The Rachael Jayne Groover tribe and how I am awakening to my impact on the world is supporting me to land more fully in the world, being able to draw on the wealth of stories, experiences, and wisdom to share via speaking and writing.

The writing tribe. I love the way Tom Bird creates retreats for people who want to write books. The experience of his writing retreats has impacted my writing significantly. Long may it continue as I continue to understand and allow my writing craft to develop.

The family tribe: I feel connected to them all and sometimes disconnected from them all. True of all connections. I have to know disconnection to know connection. I know I am learning a lot more about myself through co-parenting all my stepchildren.

"Learning to dance in the rain" is still a work in progress. When the timing is right, there will be time for the spontaneous joy expressed as a dance or perhaps a song. I know that joy is the underlying message of my soul.

LIKE-SPIRITED PEOPLE

Thomas's dad, Bill, and I moved back to Hong Kong in 1996 after we were married in New Zealand earlier that year.

In late 1997, Thomas was born. What a bundle of joy he was!

You know how the journey goes. Thomas contracted pneumococcal meningitis at the tender age of nine-and-a-half months. That sent me on a quest, a crusade to fix my baby boy. Remember, that's how I saw it then.

There were several years of rehabilitation. In truth, it will be a life-long rehabilitation from his encounter with pneumococcal meningitis and consequent illnesses.

As I have mentioned, Thomas and I explored many different therapies, talked to loads of practitioners and "alternative" believers. What was crystal clear to me is that I needed to look at this spiritual wake-up with different eyes otherwise my physical body would be fried. Thomas's system probably would not have survived, either. There was such an intensity of analysis, enquiring into the why it had all happened, blaming, and victimhood. Many of you will relate, if you want to acknowledge this. I certainly related to this way of doing life for many years. The sheer exhaustion on all aspects of my physical body and all the other bodies such as mental, emotional, social, and spiritual. After time, reflection, and much searching, a new awareness arose. Now I am conscious about the way I choose to live life. This isn't to say I don't revert to my previous unconscious self, as I am not perfect. My humanness does appear to remind me of that fact.

As I explored, I found that I wanted to be more in a community who were like-minded. Actually 'like-spirited' is a more correct word. It was about feeling my heart connection and allowing my heart a voice within this "mindy" world of mine. This challenged me. It took me ages to learn, to practice listening to my heart, as I had operated in my mind for all my life.

One day in the early 2000's, in preparation for Thomas finishing his attendance of a reverse integration (a reverse integration class is a classroom primarily for children with challenges and there was a small number of places for neurotypical children) pre-school at the Matilda Hospital, I had been guided to visit a pre-school called Sunshine House. Its philosophy was "for the love of the children." This resonated with me. I booked an appointment with the local branch in Pokfulam, Hong Kong, as it was close to our home so our travelling time would be kept to a minimum. Fortunately, it was a meeting with the school's founder, Karen Cole.

The meeting went well despite Karen wearing dark sunglasses the whole meeting. Seemed weird at the time but I found out that she couldn't find her everyday glasses. This was the start of a dear friendship. We knew we were like-spirited and came from a place of the heart. Not long after, she introduced me to a healer she had met recently, Therese Bell, as I knew Thomas was in need of some healing energy work. A friendship with Therese began, too.

After many meetings, brain-storming sessions, fun get-togethers and hours speaking to a spiritual channel we all had in common, John the Beloved, we knew we had a deeper purpose. It wasn't just about friendship, it was to create something for children with challenges. I could see Thomas was the catalyst who brought us all together to create something for him and other children with challenges in Hong Kong.

The three of us became the co-founders for The White Rose Children's Foundation (WRCF) and The White Rose Family Foundation (WRFF). The WRCF was to be the business arm and WRFF the charity side. In truth, we didn't make any money. We gave our time and money for several years. We were able to accommodate and educate Thomas and a number of other young children who had challenges, whether they be learning, physical, mental, or emotional. Also, we were able to raise funds for WRFF to provide after-school activities for children with challenges. At that time, nothing was offered at schools for children with challenges. We offered a parent support-group, mainly meeting for coffee and Krispy Crème doughnuts, supporting each other, and having interesting speakers share their perspectives on all aspects of challenges from nutrition, to exercise, to rehabilitation therapies. Each speaker benefited us in some way.

Through our connections, we found a local school that was able to assist by allowing us to use a classroom, their hall, and their roof to run classes such as nature, yoga, dance and five rhythms (a profound meditative movement practice which encourages freedom and fluidity in dance and in life). These classes were well attended, but unfortunately the funding didn't last as long as we wanted it to. On the other side of the coin, the fact that there was a need for the WRFF showed schools they were not providing after-school activities for children with challenges. What happened was, the schools that were educating children with challenges started to offer after-school activities. They had the classrooms, the space, the trained professionals and teachers. I was so thankful that the schools were now able to offer an array of opportunities and activities for children with challenges within their premises.

When I left Hong Kong in 2012, I resigned from the board of directors. I believe the charity is still in existence but not active.

Although it is disappointing that we weren't able to raise more funds, and continue our work offering after school activities, support parent groups, the fact schools were able to step up and created more opportunities for children with challenges was incredible.

At the foundation of WCRF and WRFF was our motto.

THE WHITE ROSE FAMILY FOUNDATION MOTTO

This motto was created with our charity and our beneficiaries, the children who had challenges, in our hearts.

Accept me for who I am
Respect me for who I am
Love me for who I am

I was a cofounder of this charity, and I needed to embrace this motto. After too much time, so much self-judgment and analysis, I truly got it, embodying it. The motto is now an important part of Thomas's message to the world. For when we accept, respect, and love ourselves, we are able to do the same to others.

Thomas was the catalyst for the charity Karen, Therese, and I co-founded. Thomas was indeed the one who brought us together to create the vision, the motto to facilitate the hopes and dreams for not only him, but also for other children who had challenges and needed another avenue than the 1, 2, 3's and A, B,C's.

We knew for the "ones" who had different abilities that their key to unlocking their potential was going to be from looking outside the box. It was going to be in the scope of unknown possibilities, tapping into the unknown potential.

The initial offering was courses in nature, art therapy, yoga, and hip-hop dancing for the students – and coffee and meet-up groups for parents.

I worked almost full time on White Rose Family Foundation as did one of the other directors. We were able to employ an assistant for several months, as well. Unfortunately, the funds were limited, and the environment changed, we, too, had to change. It was a time of hibernation for WRFF.

Recently, I have added 3 phrases to the motto.

I accept you for who you are; Accept me for who I am
I respect you for who you are; Respect me for who I am.
I love you for who you are; Love me for who I am

Thomas loves the additions to the motto ... so much so it is featured on his postcard.

ARE YOU LISTENING?

You do have free will. You can choose to listen, or you can choose not to listen.

It is up to you.

Here's an exercise to assist you:

Get yourself into a comfortable position. Perhaps seated with your feet on the wall or sitting cross-legged on the floor. Be comfortable.

Now close your eyes. Take deep breaths in and out. Repeat at least 3 times.

Allow yourself to bring into your mind's eye (the area between your 2 eyes ... just sense the space) a mentor, a saint, or sage, or someone whose wisdom you trust. Know that you are safe and protected, as you have your mentor with you.

Notice there are two roads/paths/doors ahead of you.

The first road is the path where you choose not to listen.

Can you see it? Can you hear it or just get a sense of it?

Walk along this road. This is the road where you choose not to listen to the one who is triggering you; it's the message beyond the behaviours, the words, the deeper message.

How is this road for you?

It's time to be honest with yourself.

How is this road really feeling? What is it looking like? Is this what you desire in your life?

Feel this, sense this.

Now come back to the start of that road/path/door and find the other road/path/door.

This road is the road when you choose to listen to that person who is triggering you, that deeper message from the best part of them.

How is this road for you?

Once again, it's time to be honest with yourself.

How is this road really feeling? What is it looking like? Is this what you desire in your life?

Feel this, sense this. What lessons are here?

Take deep breaths in and out. Repeat 3 times.

Gradually open your eyes and write down what you saw, hear and felt.

Which road are you going to choose?

I believe Thomas always invoked the strongest emotions. I have mentioned the desperation, rage, and hopelessness, as well as the connectedness, joy, and stillness, to name a few.

So, I know he is communicating through his beingness, his body actions, and his behaviours that divine presence/the universe/God is always here. Thomas, like other angels on earth and in my life, is actually assisting me to connect with that divine presence/the universe/God.

So much so it feels like it is God speaking through Thomas. Remember Thomas is non-verbal. Yet I can hear his message … it feels like it is through my heart.

The person who triggers you the most is probably trying to get across to you a message from divine presence/the universe/God.

I can tell you, you need to listen. Otherwise, the message will get louder and louder and louder until you listen. If you don't listen, you will receive a spiritual wake-up call just like me. I was so stubborn I needed several wake-up calls. I want to suggest there is another way.

The biggest tip I can give you is, listen to your body first, so STOP. Feel your emotions.

This will allow your heart to be open and more receptive to the divine presence/the universe or God's communication. Most of divine presence/the universe or God's communication came through Thomas and his communication/behaviour.

You may think this sounds weird or woo-woo or some other name you have for it. Believe me, it's true. I am sure there are many others out there who have experienced this as well.

My son, Thomas, is giving me assistance to find what I desire.

Now what path/road do you want to take?

Really, which one do you want to take?

I know when I have completed this exercise, I have taken the path of listening to Thomas. This path/road has hills and valleys, numerous mountains to climb, some with direct paths, others with zig-zag paths and others, perhaps, may have a tunnel straight through them.

Do you take the tunnel if it is offered, or do you choose to go off-road?

Whatever you do, make a choice and take a step. What to do next?

When you have one of these strong emotions, I would like to suggest you still yourself.

Process:

Feel your feet on the ground.

Imagine your legs are like tree trunks and they have roots … these roots grow from your legs into the centre of the earth.

These roots have hooks on the end so you can anchor yourself right into the earth.

Allow the energy to flow up from the centre of the earth … traveling up the roots to the ground into your feet up to your base chakra (at the base of your spine).

Allow the energy to travel through your remaining centres.

The centres are similar to the chakra system.

Your power centre (right in your reproductive organs and toward the back of the body).

Your solar plexus chakra.

Your heart centre (right in the middle of your chest near the back of your spine).

Throat chakra.

Head Centre (behind the third eye, near the back of the head).

Crown chakra (top of your head).

Raising your arms from your hips as if you are drawing bubbles with both of your arms, and reaching for the sky, bring your hands together in the prayer position, lowering your hands in front of your heart.

Visualize bringing the energy from beyond the crown back down the body into the earth again. It feels like it completes the system ... the completion of the body system.

This allows you to feel grounded in this earth while being able to connect with the greater wisdom that resides everywhere.

This is a simple daily practice. Or whenever you are feeling a bit out of sorts or feeling you can't make a step forward, this practice is a good place to start. It refreshes and reframes your body.

Then after looking after yourself, looking after your needs, Me-time, and self-care, then identify the person who triggers you ... your Thomas.

They trigger the deepest emotional states within you. You have to hear them, as the person most likely the person closest to you.

Then it is time to practice listening with your heart.

It's meditation or reflection time.

Allow your thoughts to come and go, not attaching to anyone or anything about them.

It's time for focusing on the simplest thing... i.e., breathing.

Breathing in and breathing out and repeating until you feel suitably relaxed.

Process: (Perhaps record this yourself or ask a partner to read this to you).

In this moment, get yourself into a comfortable position. Generally, I am sitting in a chair with my feet on the floor and my hands resting on my lap. (Sometimes I am lying in bed or on my couch or floor).

Close your eyes.

Take a breath in to the count of four, a short pause and then breathe out to the count of four, then another short pause.

Note: some people like to breathe in for four; hold for four; out for four, then hold for four.

One variation is breathing in for four; holding for two; out for six; hold for two, then repeat otherwise known as 4262.

You will find your rhythm with what works for you. Know that is okay.

Note: Having your legs up the wall with the 4262 is a great way to relax prior to bed. This works well for me.

Then when you are interacting with your Thomas, your loved one, ask what's really here if you are triggered?

What are they trying to communicate?

Just be curious as to what the answer will be.

Sometimes I get nothing; no words.

Sometimes I get a download of words.

In these times, where there is a download of words, I try to grab pen and paper or laptop.

Unlined paper and a gel pen are the best. Unlined paper so you can draw and write to any form you like.

A gel pen as it moves smoothly across the paper. I always use coloured pens (not blue or black), as it enlivens me. I generally choose a purple or pink. Just because I like purple and pink ... and just maybe because pink represents heart energy and purple is transformation.

I am always amazed what words are written on the paper. It's like someone else is writing through me. It's like words from Thomas. Words directly from him.

Each and every time I have deep emotions that are triggered by Thomas's behaviour, it gives me an opportunity to release that stored emotional baggage. My emotional backpack gets lighter, freer. I am getting better at not projecting on him, not blaming him, just feeling and letting the emotions go.

It's like a part of me I didn't recognise or acknowledge has been brought to my attention, and has made the unconscious conscious so it can be freed and liberated from what was held onto. Once this part is in the light, in the consciousness, I am aware.

I then have a choice to make:

- Just be aware of it or . . .
- Be aware, forgive and let go of it all, including the attachment and the story of it all.

DO YOU HAVE A THOMAS IN YOUR LIFE?

It may be obvious if you have a child who has complex, severe lifelong challenges. You may not have an obvious Thomas. Your Thomas may be a niece, a nephew, an uncle or aunt, a neighbour, a child who is at school with your child or was with you at school.

Your Thomas could be anyone who invokes emotional responses that are at polar opposites of the emotional spectrum.

Having Thomas in my life has allowed me to access the deepest desperation when I was pleading with GOD to save Thomas as he lay there in Queen Mary Hospital in Hong Kong. And then again later, when I surrendered him to GOD with a prayer from a dear friend's mother.

I experienced rage as he wouldn't stop, he wouldn't let me sleep and I wished it would all stop. I am saddened by writing this, but it's my truth.

The unconditional love you feel with your child is incredible, yet it can be so enraging at times that your physical body forgets, and you project outwardly what you are feeling.

So, who in your life pushes your buttons, causing you to project all your suppressed rage and anger at them?

Or are you passive aggressive … projecting the silent treatment?

Your Thomas will also invoke the opposite side of the emotional spectrum. They also bring you back to that place within yourself where you feel centred, love, like only opportunities and possibilities exist.

This is a place when you see the door/the path/the road where you chose to listen.

HOW DO YOU KNOW HE/SHE IS YOUR THOMAS?

You will know, as you can feel the emotion/feeling rise up within you. There is no mistaking this. I realise he is my greatest teacher. There are many wise words about our children. I am sure you have heard many of them. Here is one of my favourites:

On Children
Kahlil Gibran (1883 – 1931)

Your children are not your children.
They are the sons and daughters of Life's longing for itself.
They come through you but not from you,
And though they are with you, yet they belong not to you.

You may give them your love, but not your thoughts,
For they have their own thoughts.
You may house their bodies, but not their souls,
For their souls dwell in the house of tomorrow, which you cannot visit, not even in your
dreams.

You may strive to be like them but seek not to make them like you.
For life goes not backward nor tarries with yesterday.
You are the bows from which your children as living arrows are sent forth.
The archer sees the mark upon the path of the infinite, and He bends you with His might that His arrows may go swift and far.
Let your bending in the archer's hand be for gladness.
For even as He loves the arrow that flies, so He loves also the bow that is stable.

Chapter 4, The Prophet (Knopf, 1923)

From this realisation that Thomas took me from the depths of desperation, rage, and helplessness to the height of connection and everywhere in between, I just knew something profound was opening within me.

As I was feeling my emotions, my heart was opening more. I felt compassion and empathy even for people I felt had wronged me. My heart was operating in an unconditional way. Even the past hurts, I was able to let go of. Some of this was deeply stored resentment. Maybe you find this difficult to believe, but I could actually feel my body again. It had been so numb without me really knowing it.

As my heart opened, I began to listen to Thomas in a different way. I began to see and experience Thomas in a different way. I started to see that some of the things that trigger me no longer triggered me and the deep connectedness continued.

In this presence, we started to have more of the still moments. More moments where there are no words to describe it.

I have a photo of him and me … the Embrace of him. It's like he is protecting me with all his love and beingness. I used to see this photo as him trying to control me. Yet I knew there was love.

And this next photo I feel is Thomas is being the bridge between heaven and earth. That important bridge to connect with God and this earth we are living on.

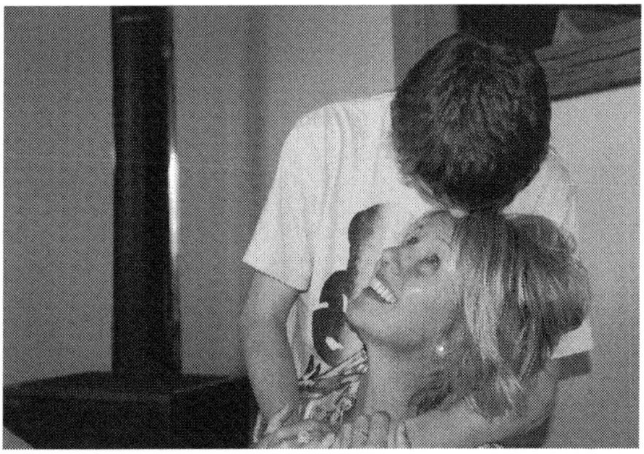

Thomas is close to me. He is my son. I had to hear him.

Who is close to you?
Who is triggering deep emotions within you?

They could just be like Thomas. They could be the conduit for the divine presence/the universe or God speaking to you. They are here to give you an important message. It's a message, an answer to your prayer, a sign, a direction, or a course correction. Whichever way you would like to see, hear, or feel it, it's a message for you.

WHO IS THE THOMAS IN YOUR LIFE?

For me, it was easy to identify my Thomas. Of course, he is the person closest to me, the one I could hear, the one who triggered the deepest, darkest, entire whole spectrum of emotion within me.

He facilitated me to accessing the depths within me. That part of me I didn't particularly want to see, feel or hear. Some may call this shadow work.

WHY IS THOMAS HERE?

I believe Thomas is here to teach me, his family, and the world that we need to listen with our hearts.

Why?

So that we can hear the words of God/the universe/the divine presence that supports us.

At a soul level, he has chosen this path for himself. The realisation of this came when I was watching Oprah back in the late 1990's when she had Gary Zukav on her show speaking about his book *Seat of the Soul.* The question was asked by a family why their child had died so young. He said so matter-of-factly … it was that soul's individual choice.

This statement resonated so deeply with me. I knew it was the same for Thomas. His soul had chosen this path, this road, this mountain for him to climb. I needed to accept that was the case and there was nothing … not a thing I could do to change that. This was Thomas's path. When I came to a place of acceptance of this, my whole world opened in a different way.

I was able to start to let go of the perceived control I had. I started to see him as perfect the way he was then I could start to see his gifts.

Through the process of trying to mother Thomas, be his nurse, his therapist, his healer, his physio, his OT, his speech therapist, I had been focused on his deficits. The things he found challenging.

I forgot to see his gifts.

His eyes that sparked hope and "I am in here."

His killer smiles.

His sheer determination.

His clarity in whether he was going do something or not.

His fight for life.

His wicked sense of humour.

His ability to feel anger in a moment and then be your best friend.

His truth about my cooking ability or lack of it at that time.

And the list goes on. You will certainly have your own list. Please do spend some time reflecting about this.

Over time and through the love, connection and acceptance of a dear friend, Tracy-Kim, we have found his gift. He is able to read people's energy and heart from their photos. He selects an oracle, angel, or affirmation card that delivers the appropriate message to his client. He has been doing this since 2012 as I described earlier.

By Thomas being Thomas, I learned to listen in a different way.

By doing this, I have connected to my true self. I have found my purposeful passion. I have found a way back to the essence of who I am, to God/the universe/divine presence that embraces me.

The way I saw it was....

God was punishing me because I wasn't good enough.

I trusted the doctors. The doctors should have known the answers.

It was the wrong advice by the wrong doctors at the wrong time and it just kept happening. This was how I saw it in the past.

No one could fix Thomas. Not even me. I felt I was at the mercy of therapists and natural practitioners and their overloaded appointment books.

We were pushed to go to New Zealand, as I lost faith in the Hong Kong doctors.

Thomas and I were separated from his father while we searched treatment and support in New Zealand.

And the list could go on.

You will have your own list of victimhood.

As time went by, I realised I was using a lot of energy being a victim … although I probably didn't express it externally as I generally was the "half-full girl," even though internally my mind was in turmoil. Analysing, what "if-ing," thinking, thinking of all the possible scenarios. And yet, there is no way my mind would have come up with where I am today.

So, I have to tell you it is a waste of time and energy trying to control, trying to fix your Thomas. It led me to burn-out, hopelessness, despair, and a load of grey hair. Thank goodness for hair colouring products as I am not ready to go fully grey. That day will come but not in my sixth decade. Maybe the next one.

What is the point? Why is Thomas here?

To wake me, you, all of us, up. To be aware that the soul, heart, and will are beyond the dimension we see, beyond what our ego and personality can comprehend. I say this as this is what has happened to me and I have witnessed it in others. Also, I see others who still suffer and struggle with their circumstances. I know they are on their journey.

As I have experienced and defeated my own struggle and suffering, I am able to feel or sense it in others. It's because I was there. I lived there for years.

The reason for writing this book is let you know there is another way. Your Thomas is trying to tell you this by whatever means he/she has. Whether this be their behaviour, their sounds and screaming, their seizures, or whatever challenges your Thomas is learning to deal with.

As I have mentioned earlier, it starts with awareness of what is, and being aware that there is another way other than struggle and suffering.

Surrendering to this moment. Accepting what is in this moment. Then finding the courage to take a step forward. It doesn't matter if it is a baby step. All steps count. I know, as I wear my Fitbit to ensure I walk my 10,000 steps each and every day. I love my Fitbit as it keeps me accountable to my physical health and wellbeing. Find a way to be accountable … a group of friends, a support group, or perhaps a mentor.

When I say wake us up, it's about allowing our minds, particularly in my case as I am a mind type personality, to rest and listen to the quiet voice of your soul. If you have a look at the Enneagram (a model of human psyche taught as nine interconnected personalities), you may be a mind type, too, or you may be a body type, or emotional type. Enneagram books will give you all the details you need to explore this and there are wonderful masters in our world who teach this work. I have found the Enneagram has supported my deepening understanding and compassion for myself and others.

As I have a busy mind, the most difficult thing I try to do is to be still … in body and in mind. That's why meditation is such a good practice for me. I really have to practice it, though, because it is not something that comes naturally to me.

Thomas has showed me by being himself that I needed to deal with my triggered emotions. He has been that angel on my shoulder reminding me

To stop
To look
To listen

And to be fully present to this moment. Thomas has used his behaviours and limited words to guide me to these simple actions. Stop, Look, Listen.

I always know when I have fully "got it," according to Thomas, as he gives me the tenderness of grins. His grin totally melts my heart and the words I hear are, "Mum, I can feel you. I sense you are fully here at this moment." Yet the words are not spoken. I know and sense that. There is no space, no time, just at one with each other.

I feel the joy of life in my heart. There is no doubt, fear or judgment that this is not real.

I know it is why my Thomas and your Thomas are here.

To awaken your inner knowingness and to remember who you are. Who are you? It is a wonderful question to ask yourself as part of your journaling and writing. You may be surprised to see where this simple question takes you. I know I was when I first asked myself this, as part of a transformational workshop weekend.

WHY BOTHER TO DO ANYTHING?

I want to be the best human I can be. Thomas is helping me be that person. As I have spent time in meditation and reflection, I have realised I am here to leave the world in a better place than when I found it. To be my unique expression of a spiritual being in human form.

Maybe you are motivated to do this, too, or maybe your motivation is something else. Give yourself some time to reflect on this.

Gandhi's quote....

"Be the change you want to see in the world." This has been a mantra of mine for decades. It is one I come back to regularly.

Sometimes we get off the road we are meant to be on.

Sometimes we climb the wrong mountain.

This is what I did. I realised I was on the mountain of materialism, wanting, and accumulating things and it was not fulfilling me in the way I wanted it to. I was lacking my purposeful passion. My life was painful and unfulfilled, so I wanted to make changes.

I needed my Thomas to redirect me and guide me. You need your Thomas to assist you to redirect to the road, the path, the mountain you are meant to be on ... the road, the path, mountain your soul planned for you to be on. So that you are being who you were meant to be. Fully you. You, being the full expression of who you are meant to be.

This is how I felt. I am now on the life road, path or mountain I was meant to be on.

I don't have any major regrets other than maybe I tried too hard or waited too long but in truth I don't believe there are any mistakes. All my experiences got me to where I am today.

I see all experiences as just that, experiences. They have assisted me to course-correct when needed, find another road, path or find the most appropriate mountain for me.

I am thankful, grateful and appreciate my journey to date. It has not been easy or seamless or graceful, as you have read.

HOW CAN YOU GET WHAT I HAVE WITH THOMAS?

First, take responsibility for your life.

Second, be self-aware of how you are feeling, what you want to change and what you desire.

Third, you need to identify who your Thomas is.

Only you know who brings out the best and worst of you. The good, the bad and the ugly… and some may add the beautiful or godly. Thomas has brought it all out of me. Even though I didn't see it as I was going through some of Thomas's challenges in daily life, hindsight and reflection is a wonderful thing. I now see that this has happened so that I could be fully me. I didn't know what I was doing but as a result of the decades of self-development, self-reflecting and deep-diving into my mind, body and soul, I am now truly and fully myself.

It starts with you.

Yes, this is the truth.

As a mother I thought it was all about my son. I really put everything aside. My life. My marriage. I was fully focused on Thomas, particularly when Thomas contracted bacterial meningitis … although as a new mother I probably had already put myself and my marriage in second priority. When the doctors said there wasn't a lot of hope for Thomas's recovery, the protective lioness within started on her journey to nourish, nurture, and enable/activate her son.

But after I totally focused on my son for several years, my life started to crumble.

I was burnt out.

I was giving energy and love that I didn't have.

I was totally depleted, because of that.

I was suffering. Thomas was suffering as well; so was my marriage and my general well-being and health.

Finally, I realised I needed to take care of me and my emotional health. I had always been active physically, but I hadn't addressed my emotional health and well-being or any other aspects of my life such as my spirituality.

Along the way I realised there were other aspects of me I had not reflected on and given my attention to.

The five aspects of health and well-being are:

Physically
Mentally
Emotionally
Socially
Spiritually

These are the aspects I have focused on now and are part of my daily practices. Many other people also include career/business/finance and family as different aspects. But I feel the five aspects have served me well. I will leave it to you as to whether you would like to add the additional aspects to your reflection and daily practices.

In relating to others, I knew I had some fantastic friends, and I felt connected to them. Yet as the years went by, I realised I was keeping some of my darkest, deepest moments away … these dark moments were buried deep within me … Thomas's dad didn't know and really neither did I. Buried deep from childhood, I now realise these unresolved issues were preventing me from doing what my heart and soul desired me to do.

It was like I had to undertake an expedition into my own being, into my mind, body, and soul ... find all the dark spots and corners and encourage my hurt, sadness, anger or whatever emotional spots there were to reveal themselves to me ... so I could forgive myself and others... so I could forgive God.

Yes, it took years for this to unfold so that I could feel free enough to express and share my heart's desire.

I have always sensed there are many roads to God/the universe/the divine embrace that support you.

I have explored so many different therapies, modalities, and techniques. Some of them may resonate with you and some may not. That is okay.

We are all unique and we find our way back to God/the universe/the divine embrace that supports you, in the way that best serves you.

Thomas was the human being who triggered me the most. He is the human being who now brings me to my knees in appreciation and gratitude for being alive, rather than the opposite, depression, despair, and total victimhood of "why me?"

Perhaps you can relate. Who is this in your life?

Back to you.

It is time to get real with yourself. It is time to be honest with yourself.

Are you living the life you truly desire or are you living a half-life? A life that is half-full, because you have suppressed some of your emotions.

I thought that by suppressing or probably more correctly not acknowledging or allowing or even trying to manage my "bad" emotions like rage, hopelessness, and fear, I would be living a great life. What I didn't realise that in suppressing my so-called bad emotions, I was suppressing my good emotions like passion, ecstasy, and joy. I need to feel them all. Then I could say I was having a full life.

MY PATH OF HEALING

So, where did I start?

I started looking after my physical aspects of health and well-being.

I have always been an active person. I love the outdoors and nature. In my earlier years, I played competitive sports like netball, basketball, tennis, and squash. Actually, I tried a lot of team sports. Nowadays, I have settled into walking in nature or by a beach. Practising yoga and stretching at home or in a small class. It was a way to get out of my crazy busy mind ...some call it your "monkey mind." My mind just didn't stop thinking about the past, the future, and analysing the best possible solution.

When Thomas and I returned to New Zealand in 1998, after Thomas's diagnosis of pneumococcal meningitis, I started to look for different therapies for him. When someone suggested something, if possible, I would generally try the therapy first. This was the case with both chiropractic and cranial sacral therapy. Initially, my aunt recommended chiropractic treatments. This got Thomas and I started on a more holistic approach to life and moving toward a paradigm of well-being. Cranial sacral therapy followed soon after, as did every other therapy suggested to me.

I tried everything.... When I include all the specialists we needed to visit for Thomas, the list includes Paediatrician,

Neurosurgeon, Neurologist, Ear, Nose and Throat Specialists, Speech therapist, Audio Visual Therapy, Physiotherapy, Occupational Therapy . . . the list can go on. Some days we had three or four appointments...not to forget three hours of daily home therapy for six days a week. (Note that Thomas had more than 40 volunteers assisting him with this Neuro-development therapy.) No wonder I burnt out. I wasn't attending to myself enough. I did have some self-care time, but it wasn't enough to sustain the way I was living my life.

Then, after hitting some brick walls and experiencing some spiritual wake-up calls, I started to look at my mental well-being and health; my emotional well-being and health; my social well-being and health and finally, my spiritual well-being and health.

It was not sequential as many of these aspects intersected.

As I turned and explored one possible therapy, then the inquiry would lead to something else ... my mind loves to keep busy and that it did.

My personality is one that likes to explore, as you can probably tell when I talk about adventures ... about journeys, life-hikes and roads and paths. Yes, it has been difficult for me to sit and be still.

I learned a lot about my personality during the self-development and self-empowerment courses I did. You may like to explore your personality types. There are wonderful courses/books on the Enneagram as I mentioned earlier. That was the particular tool I studied ... it has assisted me to have understanding, compassion, acceptance, respect, and love not only for myself but for others with whom I am in relationship, whether that be an intimate relationship, or personal or business relationship.

Having that compassion, love, and acceptance for myself and others has opened my heart to seeing and feeling other's perspectives. Having empathy for them and the circumstances they find themselves in.

There were times when I took on other people's stuff, their baggage, but as I grew as an individual and understood I am a spiritual being having a human experience, I learned how to have energetic boundaries, so I knew what was mine and what was theirs. At times this line can be blurred, especially when you are triggered by the interaction. I can tell you, though, that with time and practice the blurred lines become very clear boundaries thus giving very clear, intuitive feedback to those I relate with whether that be in a professional, personal, or intimate relationship.

It takes time.

It takes courage.

It takes a willingness to dive deep into the dark deep shadows of our being.

And it takes support, finding someone who is able to support you in a clear way.

Whenever someone mentioned a technique, a therapy or a practice I would test how it made me feel. Initially, I had no idea what that meant. I was controlled by my mind … I had no idea how to listen to my body.

The simplest technique for this is to ask yourself "What is my yes?" Your body will respond in its own way. Then ask yourself "What is my no?" If you are like me, your mind will want to discount it. I have learned to trust this. Sometimes I do not understand, I do not know why. I am learning to trust this simple technique. Why don't you give it a go? I have learned to listen to my body … to my simple yes and my simple no.

Also, I have a deep prayer to find the peace, the stillness, in a full, joyous life. I had to feel my pain, my tightness and restriction. I had to ask my pain what words/sounds needed to be expressed and what I was feeling. Then I had to listen and allow. Normally an action was required.

A sound.

A breath in and breath out and maybe again and again.

Go for a walk.

Sit still.

Allow the tears.

There are too many to list or describe. You need to listen to your body. The pain, the emotions.

You can do some of this alone but being in community, and having a mentor always supports you to do this more quickly especially when it is someone who has walked a similar road, path or on a similar journey. I have chosen to have mentors and link to their communities, meeting and making cherished friendships.

HOW DO I DO THIS?

I have daily practices that allow me to remember to look after myself first so that I can give my best to others. By making sure my energy tank is full, I have enough to give to others. Unlike the past, when I was giving from my reserves so much so, my adrenals were in distress and overloaded, and I had high blood pressure.

I can tell you now. I have normal blood pressure and my adrenals are operating normally. My mother had Addison's disease. Addison's disease is when your adrenal glands do not operate sufficiently. My mother required steroids for her energy each and every day for about 35 years. Bless her and all her life taught me. I can't believe she passed 10 years ago.

For many years, I have had daily practices that I would review on a regular basis so that I was keeping up with what was changing within me and my environment. These included walking, meditation and prayer, reading/watching/listening something inspiring, my gratitude's and appreciations, affirmations, writing in my journal or writing in general, connecting with my head, heart and power centres and aligning my body.

This was my practice, until I found that I was treating these practices like another to-do list. I realised I had started to get resentful of them. As much as I wanted to follow my intuition, I was not. I just had to tick them off. It felt like it was a "should," a "supposed to" and therefore I was doing the best for me.

It was a doing list.

It wasn't a being list.

I was a "practiced" best self. I knew what practices were serving me. I knew it was time to connect daily to my intuition and practice exactly what my body needed in that moment.

I needed to be an "intuitive" best self … to know intuitively what my mind, body, and soul needed each moment of the day and that would be my practice for that particular day. I was listening more deeply to what I needed in the moment. This was going to be my best way forward.

I would like to suggest that you try different techniques, therapies, and practices to feel into what works for you. We are all unique. Not one technique or combination of techniques is going to work the same for everyone.

One place to start is with a daily life review. Be honest with yourself as to how you are spending your day. Where are you spending time that is not fulfilling you?

For me, I realised I was spending too much time watching mindless television. I was spending too much time on social media. I was spending a lot of time partying … going out socially.

In summary, I was lacking direction, I was filling my day with things that didn't matter to me. I lacked purpose, what I really wanted to do with my life.

I asked myself, *what do I know?*

I knew I wanted to make an impact. I knew Thomas and my story could deliver hope to others.

I knew I wanted to feel like all the trauma and tragedy served a deeper purpose and I was able to deliver that.

The three ways I want to deliver hope to others:

Writing
Speaking
Mentoring

I knew I had to address all my own challenges and blocks. It was really out of the self-development and self-reflection that all of this became obvious. I am fortunate enough to have had amazing mentors, facilitators, and wise friends who have challenged me, supported me and of course, my very own teacher, Thomas, who has made me live my process. By the mere fact Thomas is my son, he has led me into deep inquiry.

So, take the time to review:

How do you spend your time?

What brings you joy?

What do you feel neutral about and what drains you?

Also, note what is important to you?

There are many tools on the internet that can assist you with looking at what you value in life. I would suggest you review these for yourself.

After all the exploration, using different tools, attending numerous workshops and working with a mentor, my top values are:

Connection with God/the universe/ the divine embrace that supports me.

Family and friends and quality time with them.

Purposeful passion and relationships that support and are aligned with this way of being.

By knowing your values and the practices within the five aspects we live our life, physically, mentally, emotionally, socially, and spiritually, you will easily be able to identify the daily practices that may be appropriate for you.

I am an Apple lady. I have a MacBook pro, iPad and iPhone so I use an iCalendar. I used to have calendar reminders to take deep breaths in and out. Yes, I use the iCalendar for this as I did not know that I needed to breathe in and breathe out. I was a shallow breather. I needed to practice breathing in and breathing out. I learned to do this consciously with the support of technology. Now the deeper breathing in and out comes whenever it is required ... when I feel some anxiety emerging; when I am about to drive across the Buckman Bridge in Jacksonville, Florida, when I have to advocate for Thomas or take a flight.

THOMAS ... THE MASTER

I have always known that our children are here to teach us. I didn't know how much Thomas would teach me.

Once Thomas had lifelong challenges, I thought I would have to be teaching, caring, and guiding him. I thought it would always be that way.

I was so wrong.

I am totally at Thomas's feet in awe of how he has managed to get me to this place.

It is a place of total surrender ... connected to my purpose, connected to my heart. I feel that I am aligned.

It's like I sit a little taller. I stand a little taller...at 5-foot-3 and a half, I almost feel 5-foot-4 inches. And I have this broad smile, which isn't just on the surface of my face. The smile is coming from the depths of my soul, my being. A smile of genuine peace and stillness knowing that I am embraced and taken care of at this deep level of consciousness.

My Thomas and your Thomas, whether they were born this way or in their unique way, or they have become this way through an accident, or medical negligence, they all have their purpose, their soul mission.

I wonder if you feel your Thomas is here to awaken you to your divine purpose and thus realise that your Thomas is being the greatest gift by doing that. The greatest gift is a selfless soul choice to assist others on this earthly plane.

Or maybe this is a new way of thinking for you.

Or maybe you feel as I did for many years, like a victim.

Yes, for years I felt I was a victim.

When I finally realised he was perfect the way he was and I didn't have to fix him, I believe the roles reversed and he became my divine inspiration, my constant inspiration and teacher, to be the best me or fully me. Note that this took years for me to realise this mentally and fully embrace and feel it within my whole being. So allow yourself the time and space to fully embrace this. Your Thomas is perfect just the way he is.

When I let go of trying to change what I couldn't change – the past – I let go of what I couldn't control – the future, I found a peace within that still brings me to the core of who I am … so much so that it brings tears to my eyes, not in sadness but in a knowingness of truth and being at home with the essence of who I am.

Thomas reminds me constantly to come back to this essence of who I am … even when I am thousands of miles away for months. I just know.

This "Peace Prayer of St. Francis" is a guiding light for me:

Lord, make me an instrument of your peace:
where there is hatred, let me sow love;
where there is injury, pardon;
where there is doubt, faith;
where there is despair, hope;
where there is darkness, light;
where there is sadness, joy.

O divine Master, grant that I may not so much seek
to be consoled as to console,
to be understood as to understand,
to be loved as to love.
For it is in giving that we receive,
it is in pardoning that we are pardoned,
and it is in dying that we are born to eternal life.
Amen.

HOW TO HANDLE YOURSELF?

Where are the rule books? Just like with parenting, there are no rule books. There may be books that offer guidelines. There may be signs from the universe. Ultimately, it is about trusting and following your own intuition. It is about trying something and feeling if it works for you.

My intuition made it clear I needed to attend to me first. Just like the safety instructions on the aeroplanes: Put on your mask first, then attend to others.

Attending to myself first meant self-care. It was something I had not thought about for years, well, since giving birth to Thomas. Becoming a mother changed everything for me. I know there are mothers out there who have always looked after themselves. Thank you for being the example. But I wasn't one of them. And when Thomas contracted pneumococcal meningitis, resulting in numerous lifelong challenges, self-care really wasn't part of my mindset or daily practices other than a walk … at least it was something I heard myself saying, so as to not beat up on myself.

It was one of those life lessons I needed to learn, albeit the hard way. At that time, the hard way was my way.

When I started to look after myself, I noticed that I was not as tired. I noticed I was not as reactive. I noticed I felt lighter and happier.

Therefore, when Thomas had a moment that would frustrate me, I didn't react so intensely.

The first way I looked after myself was searching for answers. I was searching and seeking answers from the spirit world. I wanted someone else to tell me why, how, when, etc. I was relying on someone else to guide and instruct me.

I became very interested in oracle and affirmation cards. I attended seminars about them. I even travelled overseas to attend seminars.

I joined a meditation group where we read cards and tried to make sense of what was going on in our lives. I visited many different clairvoyants searching clarity, hope, and guidance that life was going to get better and better. For the most part, I got what I was seeking, and it kept me going until I needed the next fix. Yes, I was probably addicted to the fix. And my visits supported me through a very turbulent, challenging time of my life.

If I reflect about these years of my life, I became very righteous. I preached to everyone about how life was … I was living with the angels and I had no grasp of the real world. The real world was too painful, too real, too uncontrollable. I didn't want to be there. I preferred to be with the angels. Not that I wanted to be dead, but I wanted to be floating with the fairies and angels. It felt light and fluffy, without any of the heaviness of the earth and real life.

As things became to crumble around me and within me, there was a sense I needed to address those things I had suppressed and stuffed away.

Then I needed to find a more grounded way of being.

As I have mentioned, this is when *The Journey*, pioneered by Brandon Bays, supported me intensely. I started my journey of self-discovery and self-development in a more grounded, embodied way. I still use the tools and techniques learned as I immersed myself in a year-long practitioner's programme.

That's when I learned about my emotions, my personality, and discovered some of my life strategies that had served me but no longer did.

If I go through my life timeline, I can clearly see that when Thomas contracted pneumococcal meningitis and nearly died, was one of the most transformational wake-up calls I needed to find my way back to me, my way back to God/the universe/ the divine presence that embraces me.

As I grounded to the reality of being on earth, the more I connected to God/the universe/the divine presence that embraces me, the more I was available to be in the now and therefore really listen to what Thomas wanted and needed.

It took time.

It took presence.

It took patience.

And ultimately, it took embracing and embodying Thomas's motto.

I accept you for you are. Accept me for who I am.

I respect you for you are. Respect me for who I am.

I love you for you are. Love me for who I am.

Now, I do my best at being this, remembering that I am human and sometimes my ego does get in the way. Just as we are gentle, compassionate and understanding of others, we do need to do this for ourselves. Be gentle with yourself.

I am still learning this as I know I can fall back into old habits where I judge, criticise and berate myself ... now knowing that my inner critic is slowly, and I mean slowly unwinding.

When you are taking care of yourself, there is a way that you know what to do. You trust the innate knowing you have to do what your intuition tells you to do.

What do I do when Thomas triggers me?

1. I am aware that this is happening. AWARENESS.
2. I stop.
3. S…Still myself in mind, body and soul.
4. T…Take a breath in and a breath out, allowing the exhale to be longer.
5. O…Open and observe whatever emotion I am feeling.
6. P…Practice, practice, practice.

If I get any messages or gut feelings or intuition, then I need to take that action. The key is to listen and trust this message. This is my soul speaking to me.

I know when I follow these simple steps of STOP, my reaction in that moment is not coming from a triggered place but from a clear, receptive space.

I am not saying I do this perfectly each time Thomas triggers me but it's a format I keep practicing. I am always surprised at Thomas's response when I do. That all-knowing grin is present. It's his way of letting me know I am present to this moment. Your Thomas may have a different way. I would be surprised if it is exactly the same way as my Thomas. And yet it could be.

As you practice this you will notice it will become easier and easier. Do not worry if you fall off the wagon. It will happen; that is okay. Remember not to beat yourself up. Thomas always appreciates it when I try. Appreciate that you are aware, waking up, and continue to practice, practice, practice.

HOW DO I HANDLE THOMAS?

Where are the guidebooks on how to handle the Thomas's of the world? There are some wonderful books out there on "How to raise spirited children" and the like. You will be able to find some in a Google search. Trust your instincts as to which ones you are drawn to. Purchase them. Remember to use the simple technique … "Is this a yes?" and wait for the answer. "Is it a no?" Wait for the answer. Then trust the answer. It is the truth of this moment. Know that the answer may change in the future as that is a new moment, and the answer may be different then.

What I did was try to manage or probably more correctly, I tried to control Thomas and control my life. But that didn't work out for me. Thomas certainly made it loud and clear that that wasn't the way for him.

Some time ago, I collected Thomas at his residential home. Thomas generally loved to go for a drive so I thought today wouldn't be any different. Note that I write "thought." The thought from the mind can often lead you astray. We set off in my car … it's a treat for him and I don't mind driving.

Off we went. This particular day was warm. Thomas decided he didn't want his clothes on. So, sitting in the front seat of my convertible, he starts to take off his clothes. I forget to mention his seatbelt had already come off. I wasn't parked yet, as I couldn't find a suitable place to stop. Also, at this time I send a quick prayer to God/the universe/the divine presence to keep us safe until I could find a safe place to park.

I needed to find a place where there wouldn't be too many people walking past so a side street might be perfect. I thought there wouldn't be many people around. So, there we are in the side street, and Thomas continues to strip all his clothes off. He was a young man naked, with his mother in the driver's seat.

I knew if I tried to dress him, he might get aggressive with me so in that moment, I decided to surrender to his way.

I used the window shade to block as much of the window as I could.

I could see a few people walking by, but they didn't look … phew.

There were many thoughts in my mind.

What would they be thinking?

This woman with a young man? Yes, you are right. Would they call the police?

I guess there was this part of me that wondered what I would do if I was walking past a similar situation.

I could tell my mind was going crazy, so I stopped. I took a deep breath in and let it out. I took a few more deep breaths in and out until I was in a place of full surrender.

I wasn't anxious. I was going to allow Thomas to cool off.

I looked across at him. He was happy. He was there seemingly very comfortable in his own skin, natural, cooling down. (Note that Thomas's body thermometer does run hot a lot of the time.)

I had surrendered. I could also see that as I felt my surrender, it was as if he were smiling at me.

"Yes, Mum, you have got it.

"You must surrender to this.

"You can't control this." As if Thomas were speaking to me.

We must have sat there in my car for a good 20 minutes. I was breathing in and breathing out, as was Thomas. Stillness and calmness amongst this situation in what would have looked like a very odd situation.

Then after those 20 minutes, I asked Thomas if he was ready to dress ... and he was. I assisted him to dress and off we drove in the surrendered stillness. This same situation in the past would have caused so much distress, and anger. In this case, there were moments of stillness ... acknowledging that my surrender had to come first.

I have experienced many of these types of experiences with Thomas. The key for me is to have my wits about me so I could avoid an escalation into challenging behaviour.

Even though Thomas is profoundly deaf, I still talk to him as if he hears.

Even though Thomas may be non-verbal and have a brain injury, there is a way he is sensing what is happening. This is why I am mindful of what I say and think in front of Thomas and nowadays I will be open and honest in front of him. Nothing is actually said behind his back. He still seems to know.

It has taken years to let go of the control.

Thomas has been showing me since his early teenage years, just like any other teenager. He wants to make his own choices, but I didn't always see it that way. I guess I was still wondering how could he make those choices? I had bought into the belief that he would not be able, and this belief was running in my subconscious mind. Thank goodness I was able to let that belief go.

The ongoing process of parenting continues....

Do you allow moments of calm and stillness to rise through your emotional release? Allow yourself this time to practice. You will be amazed at your Thomas's response.

After experiences like this, my mind would re-engage and try and make sense, judge, analyse, try to understand what just happened. I wanted to have validation from the external source.

It takes time to see the pattern of my mind. Now I can tell immediately when it (the mind) wants to regain its power.

Now I can smile, as I know it's just a thought and the thought will pass just like a feeling or an emotion, assuming we don't attach anything to it. Assuming we allow this moment to be this moment, not worrying about the past or what the future may hold which is just a projection of all past moments, it does pass.

I am a positive person. I see the light within a person, a situation, anything really.

I see the experience as an experience … not good, not bad.

This was not always the case. As far as I can remember I have been a positive person, always seeing a silver lining in the experience, the bigger picture. Generally, I shared this with friends and family.

At the same time, there were some experiences I allowed myself to hold on to. I wasn't able to let go of the experience or event where I felt there was injustice.

This served me in some ways, as it has motivated me to speak up when there was injustice. Other times I have been too afraid to speak for whatever reason.

These situations include:

Afraid to speak to anyone I thought had authority over me.

Thought it was part of my karma if you choose to believe in that.

Appear to have an opinion

Seen and not heard was the norm.

Must be a good girl

Must listen to others.

I know all of these beliefs have served me but what I realised decades ago was there was resentment residing in me that wasn't allowing me the freedom and choices I wanted in my life. It was holding me back. The resentment was a root of some of my life strategies that needed forgiveness.

I was resenting, not accepting a number of experiences and situations in my life.

Thankfully, though, I learned transformational tools that have allowed me to release this resentment by forgiving the situation, the people, God, and most importantly, myself.

Yes, I did believe God/the universe/the divine presence was to blame for Thomas's illness.

I appreciate so much of the journey I have been on, the mountains, the valleys, the narrow windy road, the road least travelled, and the fact that it's been my journey.

I needed to be aware something was wrong. I wanted to be somewhere else other than where I was. I had a choice to stay where I was or move toward where I wanted to be. Then I took action.

"Awareness is the greatest agent for change."
– Eckhart Tolle

Ask yourself these questions:

What is happening in your external world? What are you noticing?

What is happening internally with you?

Keep a journal about what your thoughts are, what you are feeling or sensing.

Do this for at least a week. Are there any patterns of thoughts, feelings, or common themes?

Now consider: are you happy where you are?

You have a choice to make.

Do you want to keep on the same path internally and externally?

Do you like the way you see you?

STILLNESS

I found a way to cope and build life strategies that supported me for years and decades.

It was through all of life challenges, the numerous wake-up calls, when I realised the coping and life strategies were keeping me from the very thing I desired. To belong to a community that accepted, respected, and loved me for who I am.

I feel gratitude for all that is. It was a wonderful expression of all the experiences that have been gifted to me in my several decades of life.

I feel I have been blessed to be in this experience.

There have been experiences that have broken me, broken me into pieces to the point that the pieces have taken time to reattach. The pieces have cracks, chips, lines of stress, lines of weakness, and yet when they are reconnected, there is a strength and courage that is far more than the sum of the pieces.

I used to feel broken was broken, imperfect, and had to be thrown away. But now I can see and feel that these parts are stronger, more available for life now that the experience has been had and truly felt.

It's the rebuilding, restructured, re-assembling that enables me to speak to you today. And in this process of rebuilding, there has been the re-emergence of an underlying stillness. It underpins everything. It's just there. This underlying stillness allows all emotion to be present, to be welcomed.

Not projected, not blamed, just embraced, by allowing it to move through.

All that remains is this … Stillness. It just is.

How often did I get so very involved in the games of the mind?

How often did I want to be right and want to lead others to a wisdom I knew to be true?

What I can do is to be true to myself. To be the change I want to see. Live my truth. Live my life, not the life others wanted me to live. The life I truly want.

It's about life's purpose. It's about coming back to myself, my soul's purpose so I can have a life full of purpose that not only allows my soul to sing but the joy and juice for life or as I like to call it "juju" will flow to all aspects of my being, even my ego.

In this, emotions must be allowed to flow. I have found a way that works for me, that allows me to process emotion, not store it up somewhere else to be dealt with at a more convenient time, not to be projected out at whoever is there with me or stored so I have a huge explosion at someone near and dear. An explosion like this gives away all my power within.

There are a lot of techniques, methods out there offering different ways, paths, journeys or hikes.

There is a way for us to allow just what is from this perfect moment in time. It is not what I think it was to be, it is what it is.

HOW DO YOU KNOW IT IS GOD/THE UNIVERSE/THE DIVINE PRESENCE THAT EMBRACES YOU?

You just feel it within you being. You know it's not from your mind.

It's like an a-ha moment. It's when you may get goosebumps.

It's when you want to say I wouldn't have ever thought of that.

Your whole body knows. It isn't a knowing from the mind. It's a whole-body experience. It is different for everyone.

For me, I could feel my whole heart open. There was no judgment, no analysing, nothing but LOVE.

I love this quote from the bible:

"Be still and know that I am God"
- Psalm 46:10.

I ask God, "How do I know it is you?

I sit at my computer and I wait for God/the universe/the divine presence that embraces me to answer me.

I know that my body is still.

I know that my mind is still.

There is a peace, a stillness and a oneness as I sense I am at one with all. People, things, all that my eyes can physically see and all that I cannot see.

Then I feel like God responds … the words are in my head.

"You just know."

"The words are simple and speak of simple truth."

I ask myself, "Is this true?"

The answer is in the way your body responds.

It is an internal sense.

It is an internal feeling.

It takes time and patience to allow the truth of this simplicity.

Follow your soul. It knows the way.

THAT THING THAT EMBRACES ALL

My first daily practice is to connect with the knowing that someone/something has my back. Whether I call this one/thing God, the universe, or the divine presence, there is a force that has my back, has my highest good, as it has my front as well. All of life comes through from this God, this divinity, this presence.

Trust the universe, ultimately trust yourself. I have hit many brick walls, had many wake-up calls. One of the big ones was Thomas's illness, pneumococcal meningitis, when I thought he was going to die.

Even though I thought I had a plan.

Even though I thought I had been good.

I thought because I had been good, did nothing bad, challenges would not be sent my way. I had such an idealistic, almost fantasy, way of looking at the world.

Even though I thought bad things happen, they happen to others, not me.

Even though I thought life was rosy and divine, it didn't mean divine challenges would not happen.

Even though I wanted to figure it out as quickly as possible so I could get on with it, sometimes the lesson was about my patience, so things come together in their time, piece by piece by piece.

Thomas has been and still is a wonderful Master of Teaching. Teaching me how to be in this moment in this particular moment. I didn't always see this as a gift. I struggled with the fact that Thomas was bringing up my anger, rage, and frustration. I struggled with all emotions, especially the rage, anger, shame, guilt, and fear.

It wasn't what I was meant to feel. It wasn't meant to be coming from a lady, an educated lady, a lady with a great upbringing. It was about being quiet, still, and not being heard.

So, I know how to be still. I know how to sit and listen. Listening but not really taking things in, not embodying. Not taking it in so I truly embodied it. The way I grew up was moulding my personality. The way my Mum and Dad related to each other, the way they related in life together.

"Please give up the struggle and resistance. This is what is," said the voice from within.

PART THREE

Conversations with Thomas

POST-BIRTH CONVERSATION ABOUT PRE-BIRTH

Now I will take you right back to when Thomas was in my belly. There were such high hopes about all he would be and achieve. Probably, it was more about what he would achieve in life, rather than who he would be. His dad, Bill, and I are University graduates. At that time, in the late 1990's, we were making our impact in the business world. It was bearing material fruit for us.

I knew I wanted a family, and I knew I still hadn't found what I really wanted to do in life or really, I don't think I had found my soul's purpose. It was a definite sense that I wasn't doing what I was meant to be doing, that's for sure.

Well, life has a way of sending you experiences, spiritual wake-up calls, to awaken you.

My biggest brick wall was the day I fell to the floor in the Adventist Hospital after hearing the doctors say Thomas had meningitis. I knew meningitis was bad, just not how bad and life-changing the disease could be. There had just been a cluster of meningitis cases in a suburb of Auckland, New Zealand where overcrowding was a problem. How could this be possible when there were three of us living in a roomy apartment in Hong Kong?

Thomas's illness reminded me that I had gotten off track. Note to self ...remember to watch Thomas closely as he has lessons to teach me just like all of our children.

Thomas was due on the September 12, 1997, according to my Obstetrician-Gynaecologist (OB-GYN). It was agreed that if my baby exceeded this date by a week, my OB-GYN would induce me. Not being a patient mother-to-be, I thought this was a great idea. I could not wait to have my gorgeous baby with me in the world.

Little did I know, Thomas wasn't quite ready. This was revealed to me only a year ago when I was asking him why he was so upset. He told me he actually wasn't ready for the world. He needed more time. I was astonished and saddened by this. I was not conscious enough those two decades ago to be aware of his soul, I was so focused on my individual journey, not our journey together.

So, based on the doctor's advice, I accepted my OB-GYN's advice. I was induced on September 19, 1997.

Thomas was stubborn and not keen to join us. He ended up being in distress. There was meconium in the amniotic fluid, so he arrived via emergency Caesarean at 11:13pm on September 19. Thomas Luke Clark Pearson was born. A bundle of joy.

In my recent conversation with Thomas, he told me he wasn't happy with being induced. He wanted to wait longer.

So, there was my lesson in patience, well, lack of patience. I finally received the understanding some two decades later.

My learning journey with Thomas had only just begun.

THOMAS GETS MY ATTENTION. THOMAS SPEAKS.

"The seizure which stopped me breathing was to capture your attention. You had been focusing too much on other issues and you were starting to think too much about others and not on what was best for you and I," Thomas recalled.

"I just needed to get your attention. So that evening in May 2012, at the Hong Kong Football Club, I had a seizure and stopped breathing. I am not sure why my helpers didn't tell you immediately, but they didn't. They probably thought you would blame them," Thomas explained.

This statement hits me right between the eyes and heart.

Yes. Thomas is probably right. Back then I probably had a lot of blame energy in my life. I knew I wanted to be showing up in life differently. It was a process of letting go.

"So, Thomas, may I ask you a question? You really wanted to head back to New Zealand? You actually wanted to be there rather than where you had been brought up, Hong Kong?" I asked.

"Yes. Yes. Yes," he responded.

"I knew it was time for you and me to find a new way, back in New Zealand."

"Is that why you answered Tracy-Kim the way you did with the oracle cards?" (See below the oracle cards Thomas pulled out when Tracy-Kim asked him telepathically what he thought about the move.)

"Yes. Finally, we, you, Tracy-Kim, and I were finding a way we could communicate."

"Are the oracle cards only about your communication or is it about others, too?" I inquire.

"The others will find their unique way of expressing. You just need to get this book out so other parents and carers can start to look beyond the disabilities to what their loved ones can do to express in their unique way." Thomas was clear about this as he continued.

"We all need to look beyond, for a new way, for a new way of communication, right from the heart, right to that part of you or your ego that is keeping you from being your potential."

WOW… what an insight this was for me!

"What a time we have had in New Zealand since we arrived back, Thomas. It was like you were blaming me for all that was wrong," I said.

"It wasn't that I was blaming you. It was only you I could trust to listen to what I wanted to communicate. Your intuition was correct. You were seeing my behaviour as communication and taking action based on that. I trusted you. I trusted Richard (Note that Richard was a support worker at the time). You both were looking beyond my behaviour. I know I made it very difficult and challenging, particularly for you and Richard. I needed you both to speak authentically so the real truth could be revealed."

"What truth are you speaking about, Thomas?"

"The truth that differently-abled individuals can communicate. We need an advocate, a champion who can see/read between the lines, the way things are being presented, not to take things at face value but look at things outside the box."

"I know you don't like to be put in a box or have a label attached."

"No one does. We are all uniquely gifted, uniquely challenged. I am just so pleased you are my advocate, my champion, Mum. It makes everything so much easier for me."

"Well, Thomas, this has been quite some journey to date. Quite a roller coaster, sometimes a hurricane or typhoon, as we called it in Hong Kong. Was this what you intended?"

"Well, Mum, you and I agreed on this a long time ago. It was a contract our souls made. We just knew there would be a road with blocks, challenges, joys and struggles, triumphs and hardship. It was just going to be life."

"Thomas, why did you decide to have the illness you had in this life? Why? It feels so difficult to understand. Is it really possible you actually agreed to this?"

"Yes. I did. It was part of my path and you wanted to be part of this evolution as a catalyst, a changer, or a shifter. You wanted

to help us bring in a new consciousness to our planet. I decided to be a catalyst in this in so many ways.

"For the doctors to look beyond their pedestal, the pedestal we have put them on.

For you and my dad to evolve into a changer. You have it in your blood. That's why Gandhi's quote has always meant so much to you, 'Be the change you want to see in the world.'

"Real-life challenges were there so you could experience them firsthand. It isn't something you have read in a book. It has been real for you." Thomas finally stops.

Finally, I get an opportunity to speak again.

"Why do I need to write this book? If it is best for everyone to experience first-hand, why am I here writing this book?"

"Everyone needs to know that it is possible. There are possibilities. There is potential. Beyond the box. Beyond the tall poppy and glass ceiling. All the myths need to be shattered. They have to know there is a way. It's their way. It's a process of letting go, facing fears, not holding onto the emotions and allowing them to pass through the body. The passing-through and allowing of all things, whatever they are. Whether we want to attach a label of good, bad, or ugly, in truth it is just an experience of life, an opportunity to allow growth."

"What are we going to talking about, then?"

"Your life experiences."

"How will this assist others?"

"It's the lessons and insights gained that will help them."

"I thought I was going to tell your story."

"My story is part of your life tapestry, part of your life embroidery. My story will be there within it." Thomas pauses, gathering his thoughts.

"I have found it very empowering to have oracle cards and photos as a means of communication," he continues.

"When you replied to Tracy-Kim's telepathic question, I couldn't believe it. Yet deep down, I knew. You finally proved to me that you were able to understand everything you were hearing (even though you are diagnosed as bilaterally profoundly deaf) and sensing. I guess you had been understanding everything for a long time."

"Yes, I had. I am not sure when I knew this was the case."

"From my perspective, as your Mum, you always seemed to have a knowing look in your eyes."

"You are right, Mum. It was a way I got it. I understood it even though the words weren't able to be spoken. I can understand the energy, I must say. I can see the energy.

"You know all those times I pointed up to the electric lights, the corners of the hospital rooms, I was seeing energies. I didn't know if you saw them or not. I could only use my limited spoken words to get your attention: Look. Look."

"What made them so exciting to you? You were always so excited as if whatever you were pointing at was telling you stuff. As if the energy was giving you messages."

"Yes, in a way. It was a bit of everything. I could see the energies, the leaks, the energies which weren't so helpful and energies that were hanging around with no place to go. The energy that needed some attention and then the energy could be allowed to move on."

"So, I guess you were helping these energies, then?"

"Yes."

"Is it strange I don't see what you see?"

"There are things you do see and feel, and you just haven't put enough attention on yet to see it at its fullest."

"Are you talking about auras?"

"It's a bit like auras. It's really energy flowing in the universe."

"Will we all be able to see this?"

"When the filters are clear, your vision will be a lot clearer. This can also be said about all senses of the human form."

"Filters?" I ask.

"The conditions that society, parents, family have conditioned us with. Also, all the social norms. Things that everyone deems to be appropriate, normal, and acceptable.

It is time for the normal to move. This is why we differently-abled are here and when we don't have a voice, we need to rely on the likes of you to listen to your soul and me and pass on the messages through your books and public speeches you will give."

What a message from Thomas!!

TRAUMA TO TRIUMPH

Out of each of these experiences something wonderful has evolved.

Out of Thomas's illness, I became who I am.

Out of Thomas's illness, I have met amazing people.

Out of divorce, I found parts of me that have been hiding. The divorce has actually allowed me to explore and put to rest some of those myths and beliefs I had about myself.

Out of Thomas not speaking, we have found a way from him to communicate in a way that is beyond many people's aspirations, yet in reach of others who want to open to all possibilities.

Out of all the dramas, I have found me. That part of me that I know I wasn't doing what I was meant to be doing. My true vocation has emerged, in the latter part of my life. I am a late bloomer ... just like an excellent bottle of aged red wine ... I am able to share it with others.

Out of a seizure with no breathing, Thomas and I moved back to New Zealand, where new possibilities emerged.

Out of Thomas's violent behaviour, Thomas and I found independence. A deep understanding of what independence meant for both of us.

Thomas is wanting his own home, searching for his own friends, relationships, a means of earning and just doing and making more of his own choices. Making his choices clear.

Out of Karen's passing, I was able to meet David and his family. It wasn't as though I had wished it or wanted this to happen. Karen had her journey and I had mine.

There was a GEM in each and every trauma.

PERFECT THE WAY HE IS

The moment when I finally got that I couldn't fix Thomas was memorable. Thomas was who he was.

I remember taking a walk with a dear friend in Discovery Bay, Hong Kong. We walked along the beach-front just a short walk from the ferry from Hong Kong Island. We were chatting about numerous topics. Out of the blue, she said to me, "You know, Thomas is perfect just the way he is." She looked at me for validation. I looked her straight in the eyes and said, "Yes, I know."

I stopped in my tracks. I couldn't move. I had to feel and fully acknowledge what I had just said. "Yes. I know." This was a defining moment for me. Thomas was perfect just the way he is. Not better, not worse. He was who he was.

So, the unwinding began. I, the headless chook (chicken for you who don't understand chook) began to see Thomas for who he was in this moment. I accepted him for who he was in this moment. I did that for myself, too. I was perfectly imperfect, like everyone else. The endless effort and striving for perfection were futile. It was impossible.

Who are you?

"How do you know this is you and I am not going mad?" I asked Thomas.

"You don't. Trust in that knowing this, all needs to be revealed and be open for the world to allow it to digest," Thomas reveals.

"Can we talk about your cards again?"

"Yes."

"Are you still wanting to have your card reading as a business called 'Tom's Readings?'"

"Yes. It is a way I know I am fulfilling my purpose. Getting my clients in touch with their authentic self. The self that needs to be revealed, nurtured, nourished, and generally felt safe and secure," Thomas replies.

"So, do you want me to talk about this in my talks and speeches?" I inquire deeper.

"Yes. You know how you feel when you speak your truth. You know how alive your body feels. Alive, energised, a force to be reckoned with," Thomas reminds me strongly.

"My body certainly responds to being on stage as I talk my truth, my passion, the way I am being in the world.

"The card readings have been an interesting point of polarity within your home, Thomas. They created so much separation. Some support workers want to assist you with them while other support workers were scared of them and did not want to support you with them. Continuing on, "It has really been a period of years where you have had to persist and persevere with your resolve to get the support workers and others such as management of the service provider into a place of acceptance. A place where they accept these readings were part of your communication and your world."

"This wasn't without much frustration, anger, and as they say blood, sweat and tears from both of us. The cards were obviously that important to you that you had to make sure the only people who were open and willing to put their beliefs aside were the support workers who could truly support you in your living environment. The other support workers who were not able to do this, were not able to care for you. You made this totally clear. You insisted on the highest level of integrity, a wide-open heart, and unconditional love. Your support workers, your supporters needed to resonate with your energy and creative process of how you want to be in the world. I know you really need to interview all your support workers."

Fortunately, this is what has happened. Thomas is present at a staff interview for as long as he wants to. You either get the thumbs-up and are led away by him or you don't. You are either in or out. It's not personal. Thomas is able to discern whose energy resonates with his. He is like the keeper or the custodian of the other young men, too. What a role he has taken on.

At this time, I remember Thomas had drawn a card for one of his flatmates. The message was, "Your dreams have been heard." It felt as though deep down he wanted that support worker to move on, too.

Now it was time for a new energy. It was time for empowerment. A time for these young men to step out of their young-boy trousers and be encouraged and guided into new adventures to allow development way beyond anything we ever thought was possible.

"Thomas, your commitment to your life purpose has meant that three other young men have been given an opportunity for something else to emerge within them, just like it has for you."

"This has only been part of my journey, Mum. There is still so much more to do and yet I am at peace with it all as it is."

"Oh, Thomas. What are you saying?" I ask.

"I am at peace at where everything is. I fully accept that this is where we are. I will not die with the music still inside me."

"Thomas, what else do you want me to tell the world through my book?"

"Love is the key."

"Love of whom?" I ask.

"The love of self. You have to love yourself enough that you care of yourself."

"What else do I need to tell the world? What about the ones who are silent?"

"The silent ones hear in ways other humans haven't even thought about. It's all to do with energy and the fact that everything is energy. There will continue to be advances in this."

"What about your cards? Do you want to make your own cards?"

"Sure. I will need you to assist me."

"I hope I can assist you, my dear, or I will help find someone who can."

"Mum, trust yourself. You will be able. You are the one who has never doubted my ability. You knew I had potential. You knew I had potential within me. Thank you for not giving up on me."

"That seems like an important message for others who have a loved one who has life-long challenges."

"Yes. It is.

Always accept what is. Always allow new opportunities, new hopes and dreams. Always love what is."

"Thomas, it's like an interview with you. Is there anything else I need to put in this book for you?"

"The quest of the silent ones. It is so important not to give up. Not to stop the love, the acceptance of what is.

Mum, know you have done everything possible for me."

Thomas asks me to share some of the most significant readings he has done for me.

Below is a photo of a card reading for me reminding me books are part of my life purpose. Thomas gave me this spontaneous reading a few years ago. I believe it was a reminder to get on with my writing.

At the card reading below as I started to face my fears of speaking on stage.

I received the above photo in an email from Thomas (via his support workers) just before I was going onto stage at the

Awakened Speaker Training in 2018: "Talk about your feelings" ... "One step at a time." I believe this was an essential step toward my big dreams coming true.

"Yes. Include all the readings you feel would motivate people to act and trust the guidance given," he said.

"Okay, I will do this. I believe I have mentioned all the significant ones. Each and every reading is meaningful. The ones I call significant, stopped me in my steps. Their impact on me touched and reacted with the core of my being, my soul."

EMBRACE OF ALL OF LIFE.

"There are no good or bad experiences. It is all of life's experiences. These experiences are all your unique experiences of life that have given birth to a book like this. Like you have said, you have experienced most of life's most stressful experiences and not only defeated them but are thriving and spreading the word. You have the way to share the voice and the words to live your joy and live your love in this.

"The timing is perfect. It is exactly where you need to be for the birthing ...you are grounded and connected. You are the perfect conduit for this type of book. After the dramas of life and writing about them, you are willing to share. It was obvious you are ready to share with others close to you but others. To be the change in the world," Thomas said.

THE MESSAGE FROM WITHIN

From deep within, I hear this message: "This is the truth of it. This is the total reality of truth, in this moment. You were born for this. The path you have been on, allowed you the knowledge of this. This is what is to happen. You have given yourself the time and space, Thomas has given you the time and space, David has given you the time and space."

Now I know I have the time and space to allow this to unfold.

"It is time now to share your experiences, your love and joy." continues the voice from within.

LIVE WITH JOY AND CELEBRATE

Before David and I married, we spoke about giving all our guests a gift. I enjoy celebrating and the drink I associate with celebrations is champagne, so champagne flutes were decided on.

We also wanted to personalise the champagne flutes. So, we came up with this quote.

"Live with joy and celebrate." We created our own logo as a way to honour the light in each other:

LEARN TO LIVE AGAIN

You have a choice now in this moment.

You can choose to listen to your heart or not. What do you choose?

You can choose to follow your soul or not. What do you choose?

Your soul knows the way. All you need to do is listen and take action.

It is time to learn to live again.

I even co-wrote a song about learning to live again. Here is the link https://www.youtube.com/watch?v=gFHolopCbkc

GRATITUDE AND ACKNOWLEDGMENTS

To the practitioners who gave Thomas and me hope. They shone a light on the next step to give us the courage, the energy to make that next step even though it was the path least followed. They trusted my intuition before I trusted it. They knew I was there in front of them for a reason. Thank you wholeheartedly.

To my friends who are walking this path with me. Thank you for sharing this journey with me. Through the mountains and valleys on the hike of my life. Thank you for shining a light when I was not able and being there to hold my hand. My heart is full with your love, respect and acceptance. I love you.

To the friends who were part of my journey and are no longer. I acknowledge all the beautiful souls who have been on this journey with me so far. I apologise if things haven't turned out the way you wanted. I know that at times my ego wanted different things, too. Know that I appreciate the journey we were on together and the influence you have had on my journey.

No regrets.

No excuses.

No justifications.

I was who I was then and now I am who I am now.

Please meet me freshly as I will meet you freshly.

Being in a place where I have no regrets, I have full acceptance, compassion, and understanding for where I am. May that be a motivation for you to get real about your life.

Just maybe your greatest fears will be your greatest teachers.

My fear of public speaking.

My fear of writing a book.

My fear of being the light by which others can see their way.

As Marianne Williamson says…

**"And as we let our own light shine,
We unconsciously give other people permission
to do the same.
As we're liberated from our own fear,
Our presence automatically liberates others."**

Thank you for being part of my journey. I am forever thankful our paths have crossed.

To my partners who have walked part of my love journey with me, I am thankful for all our shared experiences. You have shaped "the me" writing this book.

Thank you to my editors, Idony Lisle, Bill Worth and Hilary Foged for your honest feedback and skill and guidance to assist in the manifesting of this manuscript.

Thank you to Rachael Jayne and Datta Groover and Tom Bird who have nurtured and encouraged me to explore the depths within me. Writing has definitely been important in my healing journey.

To my mum and dad who have supported me in ways they were able, ultimately guiding me to who I wanted to be and how I wanted to live my life, I am eternally thankful for each of you. May you both Rest in Peace. I love you.

To my loving David who has supported me in this birthing process of this book … the time away from him and family to write, the early rises, the endless technology questions and "just give me some perspective" questions. Your love, support and sense of humour have assisted through this sometimes-challenging birthing process. Thank you for being you so that I can be me.

To Alicia, Siân and Greg: thank you for accepting Thomas and me into your family. You have taught me that unconditional love is beyond DNA. I am blessed to be able to co-guardian you with your dad.

To Thomas ... there are no words to express the feelings I have. You are a priceless gift to me, a gift that keeps giving. All I need to do is to STOP. Surrender. Accept.

To the reader ...This is my disclaimer. Everything I have shared in this book is shared from my perspective. It is the way I have remembered and processed the events in my life. My hope is you use my stories and processes to assist you in your life so you can learn and start to live again.

APPENDIX

I truly believe that every technique and practice I have researched and experienced over the decades have been instrumental in assisting me to be where I am today.

The techniques and practices have assisted me to not only connect with myself but connect with God/the universe /the divine presence and connect with others, in an authentic, open and loving way. Also allowed me to heal and move forward from childhood traumas, suppressed emotions and any other conditioning that no longer serves me.

These include:

THE JOURNEY PIONEERED BY BRANDON BAYS

https://www.thejourney.com
As it states on their website, "The Journey is a cutting-edge transformation and healing method pioneered by internationally acclaimed, best-selling author, speaker and mind-body-healing expert, Brandon Bays.

It offers a uniquely potent set of tools for awakening and liberating our infinite human potential."

THE ART OF FEMININE PRESENCE BY RACHAEL JAYNE GROOVER

https://theawakenedschool.com/events/
As stated in the Awakened School website *"Art of Feminine Presence®* is not about igniting your hot, erotic, sassy power as much as **learning to consistently embody a deep, grounded, feminine confidence that cannot be shaken by anyone or any situation.** It's a quiet stillness that everybody sees without much effort on your part and is extremely magnetic."

HEART IQ BY CHRISTIAN PANKHURST

https://www.heartiq.org/
The website states that, "Heart iQ is a way to deepen your connection with yourself, your intimate relationships and the world around you, by doing your inner work with others in community and in connection.

When we practice Heart iQ together, an amplified field is created providing an environment that is filled with profound insight, nourishing intimacy and deep healing.

Heart iQ exists to help shape a better world for future generations to come. That's' why we believe the greatest gift you can give to a world, is to become a fully healthy you."

DONNY EPSTEIN

https://epienergetics.com/
EpiEnergetics is a revolution of how people, businesses, communities and the spaces connecting us interact, collaborate, evolve, and express their authentic signature in the world.

It uniquely applies energy and information consciously and ecologically to produce your personal or organizational extraordinary.

You can effortlessly experience, harness, and evolve the energetics that shape your life, health, relationships, business, and reality…as you know it.

THE RECONNECTION BY ERIC PEARL

https://www.thereconnection.com/
The RHE is the experience of healing that is accessible by everyone and not limited to the physical, mental, emotional or religious... as it is ***infinite*** in nature.

"It's God, Love, Universal Intelligence, modulating in the sensation-frequency of Energy, Light & Information® known today as the Reconnective Healing Experience"
- Dr Eric Pearl and Jillian Fleer

SHADOW WORK

I like the way this website describes shadow work.
https://www.yummymummykitchen.com/2021/07/30-shadow-work-prompts.html

"Shadow work involves unearthing the hidden and suppressed aspects of yourself otherwise known as the shadow. It is the practice of introspection whereby you work through the darker, hidden parts of yourself. These repressed and rejected aspects of your being are what we are most ashamed about and avoided dealing with. Though it may sound terrible, everyone has a shadow side. Acknowledging that it exists comes from a place of strength, it is important to notice and recognize self-sabotaging behaviour and habits that could potentially hold you back."

As well as these teachings, I have learned to have daily self-care and soul-care practices. These include breathing, journaling, meditation/prayers and being present, along regular wellness visits to my health professionals such as cranial sacral therapist, acupuncturist and a bunch of spiritual teachers and healers.

One to one mentoring

To date, I have worked with a handful of mentors privately. I have found them invaluable over the past decades. I appreciate you and I value your love, wise words and patience. Thank you, Bill MacLeod, Rachael Jayne Groover, Morrighan Lynne, Jeannette Claire Flynn, Sharla Brown, Jacquie Sommerville and Sandy Geroux.

NICOLA'S OTHER PUBLISHED BOOKS ARE AVAILABLE ON AMAZON

About Communication...His Way by Nicola Irvine

Nicky's passion overflows as she shares her knowing that people are social beings and have a deep need to connect with each other; every individual deserves to be heard regardless of the way they reach out to others.

"As the tears poured, I noticed that my thoughts and emotions clarified. I felt I would rather die than speak the truth about what was happening with Thomas:

- I feared he would be taken away from me.
- I feared doctors would drug him so I would not know who he was.
- I feared his spirit would be lost to the world of medicine.
- I feared that I was not a good mother." Nicola Irvine

If you relate to these comments, rest assured you are not a bad mother and your child/ren are perfect just the way they are. Yes, your life is an endless test of love, patience, endurance and insights and you are not alone.

If you or someone you know is living with children with disabilities, this book will reassure them that there are others experiencing their fears, frustrations, insights and hopes and living continually with shaken equilibrium and stress.

Communication His Way is guaranteed to make you laugh, cry, giggle and be absolutely amazed about Thomas's journey and growth.

Communication
...his way
Nicola IRVINE

ABOUT TRUST LIFE'S JOURNEY BY NICOLA CLARK

In this honest and at times raw and emotional account of the story of a young boy called Thomas, you will read a first-hand account of a mother's journey and the struggles and triumphs of living with a boy with disabilities.

Nicola shares the highs and lows of her extremely challenging yet at the same time empowering life which she has travelled with her inspirational son Thomas. A journey which has been the catalyst for her to face her fears and awaken to the truth of her inner self. Over time she came to see Thomas as a gift enabling her to become the individual she was born to be.

This book has been written to assist others facing similar situations or those who often ask, why me when things don't go to plan. Nicola has been willing to share her vulnerability from the perspective of an individual who has learned through pain to speak and write openly from the heart. In doing so she empowers others to do the same.

In addition, many of the people in Thomas's life have contributed their experiences to the book and the transformative effect Thomas has had on their lives.

This book will at times make you laugh, cry, empathise, be astounded and humbled as you share the experience of a mother's inner strength, knowing and love for her inspiring and courageous son Thomas.

trust life's
JOURNEY
the struggles and
triumphs of living with
a boy with disabilities
Nicola CLARK

Speaking Engagements and Book Launches

Nicola is available to speak at conferences, seminars and corporate events about her extraordinary journey.

She is also available for book readings and launches in your region.

For more information and to discuss your specific requirements, availability of dates, etc. please contact via email nicola@nicolairvine.com.

ABOUT THE AUTHOR

Nicola Irvine (nee Clark) was born in New Zealand then subsequently lived in multiple countries including Hong Kong, Florida, USA and Scotland.

She first worked as a chartered accountant for Ernst & Young, Broken Hill Proprietary and HSBC. Although a respectable and financially rewarding career it was not until her life was completely turned upside down by unforeseen circumstances that she discovered her true vocational passion.

A passion that began out of a situation of sheer agony when in 1998 living in Hong Kong, she learned that her beautiful, perfect 9-and-a-half-month-old son contracted meningitis, leaving him with bilateral deafness, epilepsy and global delay, to list only a few of his many challenges. It was then that Nicola's life took on a whole new role, that of being a mother to a boy with "challenges".

Despite a dim prognosis and doctors who saw little hope for improvement in his condition

Nicola had no intention of giving up on her son. She began a marathon of therapies, traditional as well as alternative ways to achieve any amount of improvement and shared these methods, hopes and dreams with like-minded groups, several which she herself initiated, all in the hopes of sharing and assisting others in similar circumstances.

The enormous impact of what happened to her son Thomas took on a surprising life of its own, one which was rich in opportunities she could never have thought possible. She could now at long last see the situation as a priceless gift to make a difference in the way individuals with challenges are perceived and treated in society.

In 2006 Nicola co-founded 'The White Rose Family Foundation' (WRFF), a registered Hong Kong charity that worked effortlessly to integrate children with mental and physical challenges into the community. For 7 years WRFF successfully funded various developmental courses and after school activities through raised funds and charitable donations.

Whilst in Hong Kong, Nicola served for 3 years as a Community Member on the West Island School council in Hong Kong. As well as serving 3 years on the English Schools Foundation Board of Governors, Hong Kong.

Nicola works as a trained Journey Practitioner. 'The Journey' is a process that assists individuals to unblock emotional issues which may be stunting their full potential. Nicola's own past Journey work assisted her greatly in being far more open and truthful. In turn, reaching out to others with an open heart has acted to amplify her levels of compassion and love for all those seeking a way to experience joy even through adversity.

Now living back in New Zealand with her husband, David and their 4 children, Nicola has a practice called Silent Gifts. Through "Silent Gifts" she helps professional parents who struggle with fear, exhaustion, and feeling like they're on a hamster wheel, to finally experience calm, clarity and peace so they can have a happy, joyful home life.

Nicola understands well the 24/7 nature of the job, caring and living with a loved one with disabilities/challenges. It can be an emotional roller coaster, and know you are not alone even though you feel it at times.

Please connect with her via email nicola@nicolairvine.com. Her website is https://nicolairvine.com/.

To connect with Nicola's son, Thomas via email tomsreadings@gmail.com. His website is https://www.tomsreadings.com/.

Made in the USA
Columbia, SC
12 May 2022

60309689R00146